BARACK OBAMA

BARACK OBAMA

His Legacy of Hope & Change

BY KATHLEEN PERRICONE

CENTENNIAL BOOKS

8

52

112

126

154

166

LASTING LEGACY

When Barack Obama was elected the first African American president of the United States on November 4, 2008, history was made. "It's been a long time coming, but tonight, because of what we did on this date in this election at this defining moment, change has come to America," marveled the young politician, who overcame a largely unstable childhood—abandoned by his father and raised by his grandparents in Hawaii—to become the leader of the free world.

As president, Obama promised to solve the health-care crisis, improve education, end the Iraq War and reshape an American economy devastated by a recession. And during his eight years in office, he made good on much of his word: He created jobs and reduced unemployment; introduced Obamacare; brought soldiers home from the Middle East; spoke out on gun control; supported the legalization of same-sex marriage; and ordered the operation that resulted in the death of 9/11 mastermind Osama bin Laden.

And America got not just a determined president, but also an inspiring first lady in Michelle Obama. Not only was she her husband's biggest support system in the White House (and devoted mother to their daughters, Malia and Sasha), but she also made her own mark with passion projects like Let's Move!, her initiative to get children healthy. "Michelle never asked to be first lady," noted President Obama. "But I always knew she'd be incredible at it and put her own unique stamp on the job. That's because who you see is who she is—the brilliant, funny, generous woman who, for whatever reason, agreed to marry me."

When the Obamas left the White House in January 2017 and returned to civilian life together, it was the enduring strength of their 25-year marriage that most impressed (and relieved) the 44th president. "The first thing that went through my mind was, sitting across from Michelle, how thankful I was that she had been my partner through that whole process," revealed Obama. "And for us to be able to come out of that intact—our marriage is strong, we're still each other's best friends, our daughters are turning into amazing young women—the sense that there was a completion and that we had done the work in a way that preserved our integrity and left us whole, and that we hadn't fundamentally changed, was a satisfying feeling."

PERFECT MATCH
"I couldn't have done anything that I've done without Michelle," the president said of his first lady (they're seen here disembarking from Air Force One on August 10, 2013). "I count on her in so many ways, every single day."

A NATURAL LEADER

A LOOK BACK AT BARACK OBAMA'S MOST MEMORABLE MOMENTS, FROM HIS PRESIDENTIAL CAMPAIGN AND HISTORIC WIN TO HIS GREATEST ROLE—AS HUSBAND AND FATHER.

BARACK FAN CLUB
"I am one of his biggest allies," Michelle (here, snuggling up to Obama on March 27, 2015) said about her husband. "I am one of his biggest confidantes."

NEVER FORGET
President Obama, the first lady, Vice President Joe Biden and second lady Jill Biden led a moment of silence on the White House's South Lawn, to mark the 12th anniversary of the September 11 terrorist attacks, in 2013.

TRUE BROMANCE
Joe Biden said Barack Obama is "a man I'm proud to call my friend." They shared a laugh in 2010.

KIDDING AROUND
The president played with Ella Rhodes—the daughter of Deputy National Security Advisor Ben Rhodes—who was dressed as an elephant for a White House Halloween event in 2015.

"ABOVE ALL, CHILDREN NEED OUR UNCONDITIONAL LOVE—WHETHER THEY SUCCEED OR MAKE MISTAKES."
—Barack Obama

REMEMBERING SELMA
The Obama family, including Michelle's mother, Marian Robinson (holding her granddaughters' hands), commemorated the 50th anniversary of Martin Luther King Jr.'s civil rights march in Selma, Alabama, on March 7, 2015.

PICTURE PERFECT
For the Obamas' family portrait in December 2011, they posed in the Oval Office after returning home from church.

"I'M STILL PRACTICING, I'M STILL LEARNING, STILL GETTING CORRECTED IN TERMS OF HOW TO BE A FINE HUSBAND AND A GOOD FATHER."

— Barack Obama

FIRST GENTLEMAN
The president gave his wife his suit jacket to keep her warm after an inaugural ball on January 20, 2009.

MOVING FORWARD
On November 4, 2012, two days before the election, the president campaigned in Hollywood, Florida—a state he went on to win.

PROUD PAPA
Obama and Michelle congratulated Sasha after she scored a hole in one during a miniature-golf game in Panama City, Florida, on August 14, 2010.

"ON THE COURT I COULD FIND A COMMUNITY OF SORTS, WITH AN INNER LIFE ALL ITS OWN."
—Barack Obama

WHOLE NEW BALL GAME
Senator Obama, who played basketball in high school, shot some hoops at Riverview Elementry School in Elkhart, Indiana, on May 4, 2008.

COMMANDER IN CHIEF
The president received a warm greeting from troops at Bagram Airfield in Afghanistan on May 1, 2012.

HALLOWEEN TREAT
Obama was charmed by a little boy dressed like Pope Francis at the 2015 White House Halloween celebration.

MASS APPEAL
Obama met with Pope Francis in the Oval Office on September 23, 2015, on the pontiff's first visit to the U.S.

FOUR MORE YEARS!
The president and first lady were all smiles as they rode to his inauguration on January 21, 2013.

SEAL OF THE PRESIDENT OF THE
STATES

NUMBER 44

“ONE OF THE BEST INVESTMENTS WE CAN MAKE IN A CHILD’S LIFE IS HIGH QUALITY EARLY EDUCATION.”

—BARACK OBAMA

READY FOR A CLOSE-UP
POTUS had fun playing with the kids in a pre-kindergarten class in Decatur, Georgia, on February 14, 2013.

RACE YA!
Obama had fun with Sarah Froman, daughter of National Security Advisor Mike Froman, in the Oval Office on July 9, 2012.

PUPPY LOVE
Obama played a game of football with the first dog, Bo, on the White House's South Lawn on May 12, 2009.

RIDING HIGH
Candidate Obama had a blast with daughter Malia (left) at the Iowa State Fair on August 16, 2007.

FUN IN THE SUN
Sasha and Obama frolicked in the ocean on a trip to Panama City Beach, Florida, on August 14, 2010.

"THAT'S WHAT BEING A PARENT IS ALL ABOUT—THOSE PRECIOUS MOMENTS WITH OUR CHILDREN THAT FILL US WITH PRIDE FOR THEIR FUTURE."

—Barack Obama

ROYAL TREATMENT
Prince George, the eldest son of England's Prince William, was allowed to stay up late to meet President Obama, who gifted him with a rocking horse, on April 22, 2016, in London.

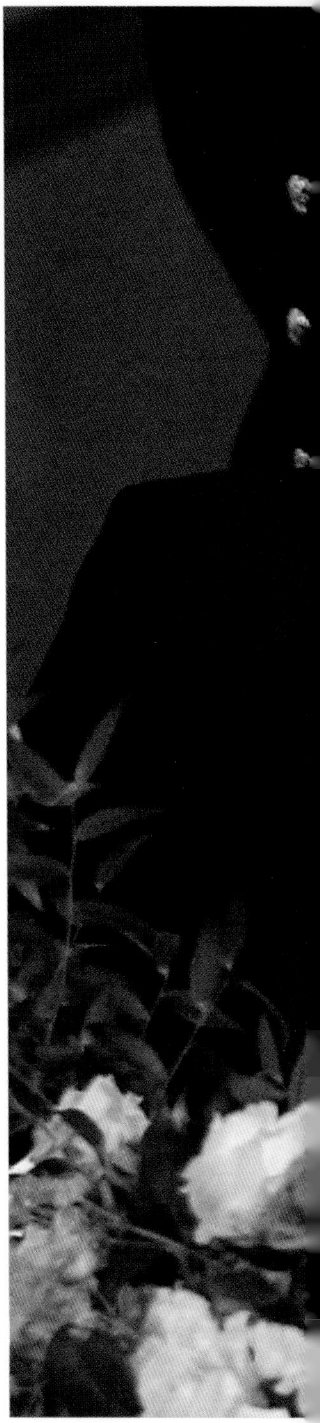

COURTING THE QUEEN The president and HRH Elizabeth II enjoyed a State Banquet at Buckingham Palace on May 24, 2011.

BEST FRIENDS
"It has to be a true partnership," Michelle said of marriage. In March 2011, the couple shared a moment in the White House Blue Room before an official event.

"THE QUALITY I LOVE MOST ABOUT HER IS, SHE'S HONEST AND GENUINE."

—Barack Obama, about Michelle

WILD RIDE
The first couple hitched a ride on a golf cart at an inaugural ball on January 20, 2009, in Washington, D.C.

FAMILY TIME
The president and daughter Malia took a bike ride during an August 2013 vacation on Martha's Vineyard.

"ANY FOOL CAN HAVE A CHILD. THAT DOESN'T MAKE YOU A FATHER. IT'S THE COURAGE TO RAISE A CHILD THAT MAKES YOU A FATHER."

—Barack Obama

GOT YOUR NOSE!
Obama found a young fan during the U.S. Embassy greeting in Prague, Czech Republic, on April 4, 2009.

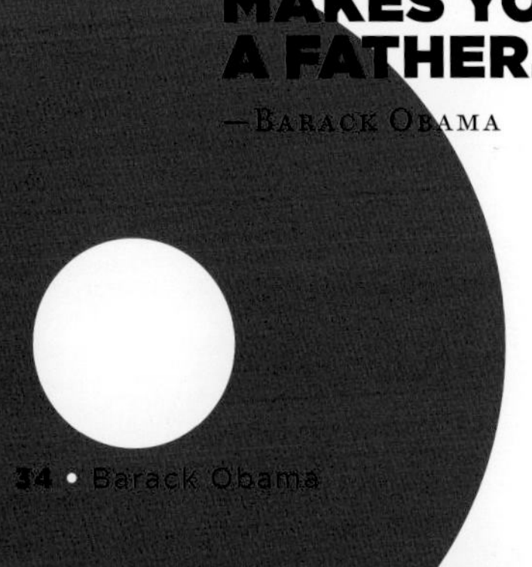

FUEL FOR THOUGHT
The president snacked on a nectarine following a town hall meeting in Bristol, Virginia, on July 29, 2009.

BEAR HUG
Obama held Jimbelung the koala before the start of the G20 leaders' summit in Brisbane, Australia, in 2009.

"OUR MOST IMPORTANT TASK AS A NATION IS TO MAKE SURE ALL OUR YOUNG PEOPLE CAN ACHIEVE THEIR DREAMS."

—Barack Obama

WINDOW OF OPPORTUNITY
The president greeted children at a day care facility near his daughter Sasha's school on June 9, 2011.

"NOT IMPRESSED!" Gymnast McKayla Maroney and Obama put on her expression that went viral during the 2012 Olympics, where she won a silver medal for the vault.

JOY RIDE At the 2007 Iowa State Fair, Senator Obama and Sasha grinned through a bumper car ride.

SUPER BOWL SUNDAY
The Obamas and their guests wore 3-D glasses to watch a Super Bowl commercial during a party at the White House on February 1, 2009.

GOTCHA!
Obama got caught in Spidey's web when Nicholas Tamarin was trick-or-treating with his dad, White House aide Nick Tamarin, on October 26, 2012.

"CONTRARY TO THE RUMORS…I WAS NOT BORN IN A MANGER. I WAS ACTUALLY BORN ON KRYPTON AND SENT HERE BY MY FATHER JOR-EL TO SAVE THE PLANET."

—Barack Obama, joking in 2008

WEST WING MAN
"I believe in change because I believe in you, the American people," Obama, here at the White House, said in 2016.

PRIMARY COLORS
Before the Nevada primary in 2008, presidential candidate Obama spoke at a campaign rally in Reno.

SATURDAY MOURNING
Michelle looked on as the president hugged a woman at Arlington National Cemetery on September 10, 2011.

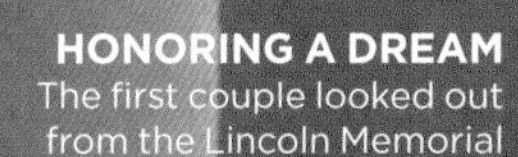

HONORING A DREAM
The first couple looked out from the Lincoln Memorial on August 28, 2010, the 47th anniversary of the March on Washington.

TENSE TIMES
National Security Advisor Susan Rice and Obama received updates on a terrorist attack in Belgium on March 22, 2016.

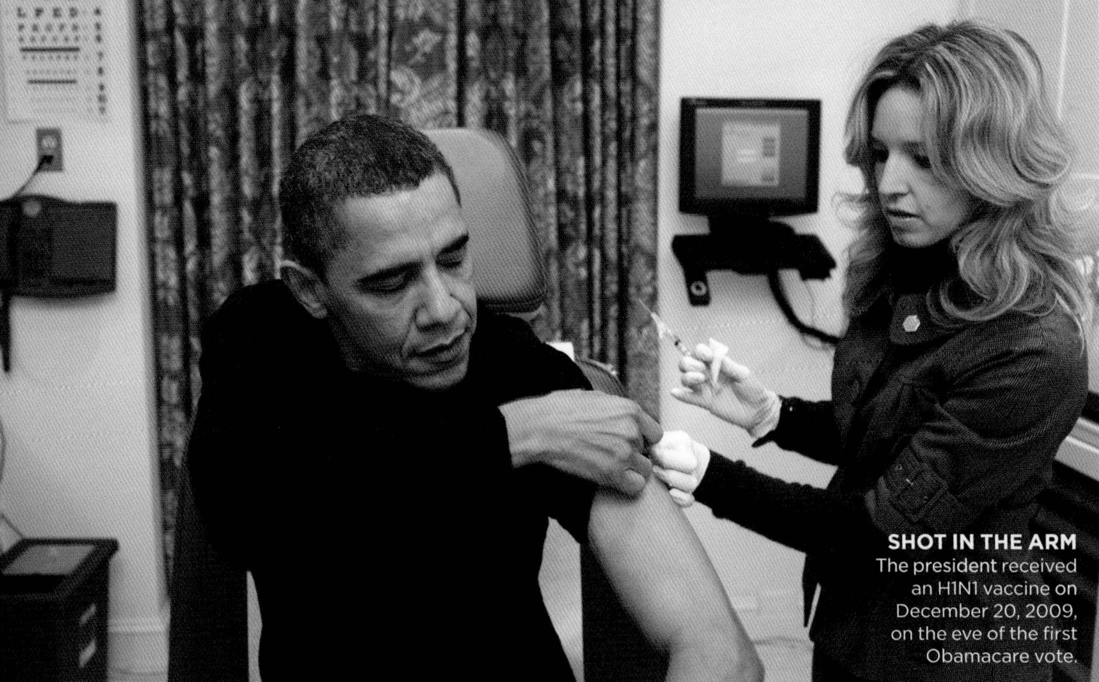

SHOT IN THE ARM
The president received an H1N1 vaccine on December 20, 2009, on the eve of the first Obamacare vote.

FLYING HIGH
Obama checked out the view from Air Force One during a November 17, 2011, flight from Canberra to Darwin, Australia.

WORLD TRAVELER
On a trip to Egypt, Obama visited the Great Sphinx of Giza and the pyramids on June 4, 2009.

TIME FOR PLAY
Obama and Biden practice their putting skills together on the White House green in April 2009.

"IS THERE ANYONE OUT THERE WHO STILL DOUBTS THAT AMERICA IS A PLACE WHERE ALL THINGS ARE POSSIBLE?"

—BARACK OBAMA

SHARP-DRESSED MAN
The president got ready for the annual Alfred E. Smith dinner in support of the Archdiocese of New York on October 18, 2012.

CAMP COUNSEL
The president studied a briefing at Camp David in Maryland on October 21, 2012.

"CHANGE WILL NOT COME IF WE WAIT FOR SOME OTHER PERSON OR SOME OTHER TIME. WE ARE THE ONES WE'VE BEEN WAITING FOR."

—Barack Obama

LITTLE BOY LOST

OBAMA WAS BORN IN HAWAII TO A BLACK FATHER AND WHITE MOTHER, BUT RAISED BY HIS MATERNAL GRANDPARENTS—CAUSING HIM TO STRUGGLE WITH ISSUES OF ABANDONMENT AND RACIAL IDENTITY WHILE GROWING UP.

"A lot of my early memories are of an almost idyllic sort of early childhood in Hawaii," recalled Obama (seen here as a boy in Honolulu).

"THERE WAS ONLY ONE PROBLEM: MY FATHER WAS MISSING. HE HAD LEFT PARADISE, AND NOTHING THAT MY MOTHER OR GRANDPARENTS TOLD ME COULD OBVIATE THAT SINGLE, UNASSAILABLE FACT."

—Barack Obama

L

LONG BEFORE HE MADE HISTORY as the first black president of the United States, Barack Hussein Obama II had already overcome so much adversity in his life. Not only was he born to a white woman and black man during a time when segregation was legally keeping the races apart in America, but growing up, his parents' relationship was so strained that he had hardly any contact with his father. And after being bounced around Seattle and Indonesia with his mother, he was eventually raised by his maternal grandparents in Honolulu. Although the couple did their best, nothing could replace his desire for a stable home life with two loving parents. "You see, I spent much of my childhood adrift," Obama explained in a 2008 speech. "My father left my mother and me when I was 2. My mother remarried, and we lived in Indonesia for a time. But I was mostly raised in Hawaii, by my mom and my grandparents from Kansas. Growing up, I wasn't always sure who I was or where I was going."

It was a twist of fate that brought his parents, Barack Obama Sr. and Stanley Ann Dunham, together in September 1960, when both University of Hawaii students signed up for the same Russian 101 class on the Manoa campus. Barack Sr. was a 26-year-old foreign student from Kenya (the college's first-ever from an African nation) in his second year, while Stanley—or Ann, as she preferred to be called—was only 17 years old and had just arrived on the island from Seattle—a move her father, Stanley Dunham, had forced her to make with the family when he got a new job with a furniture distributor. Ann had desired to remain in Seattle and attend the University of Washington; but because she was still underage, she had no say in relocating to Hawaii, which just a year earlier had become the country's 50th state. "It's paradise, for Christ's sake," Stanley yelled at his teen daughter when she challenged his authority. "Everyone wants to live in Hawaii!"

Although little is known about the beginnings of Barack Sr. and Ann's romance, in early November 1960, less than two months after their first day of Russian class, she became pregnant with their child. On February 2, 1961, shortly after the students took their final exam, they boarded a quick interisland

"WHEN BARACK SMILES, THERE'S JUST A CERTAIN ANN LOOK. HE LIGHTS UP IN A PARTICULAR WAY THAT SHE DID."

—Nancy Peluso, Ann's friend

A 2011 biography on Barack Sr. claimed he and Ann had planned to give up their boy for adoption when he was born.

flight from Honolulu to Wailuku, on Maui, to get married, with no friends or family present. But once husband and wife, not much changed in their relationship. Despite being 18 and a married woman, Ann still lived with her parents, while Barack Sr. kept his own apartment in town. Another layer to their unconventional relationship: Barack Sr. had a wife and two children back in Kenya, whom he had abandoned for an American education. But when University of Hawaii foreign-student adviser Sumie McCabe confronted him about his double life, Barack Sr. insisted to her that in his native country, "all that is necessary to be divorced is to tell the wife that she is divorced—and that constitutes a legal divorce," according to McCabe's report with the U.S. Immigration and Naturalization Service, to whom she had reported Barack Sr.'s unscrupulous behavior.

The strange living arrangements continued until the newlyweds welcomed their son on August 4, 1961, at 7:24 p.m.—two years to the day (and almost to the hour) since Barack Sr. had boarded a flight out of Nairobi bound for his new life in America. Despite the less-than-ideal situation, Ann's parents, Stanley and Madelyn, were thrilled to be grandparents and excitedly called their family members with the good news. "He's not black like his father," is how Madelyn described her new grandson to her younger brother Charles. "He's not white. More like coffee with cream."

The Last Time He Saw His Father

After nearly a decade away, Barack Obama Sr. returned to Honolulu in December 1971 to spend time with his 11-year-old estranged son—and their month together was a mix of highs and lows. When the Harvard graduate was invited to speak to Barry's fifth-grade class about Kenya, the little boy was nervous; but his anxiety faded once his father's entertaining tales impressed everyone. "He seemed to be real proud," recalled classmate Pal Eldredge, "right at his side, kind of holding on to his dad's arm." Another student gushed to young Barry, "Your dad is pretty cool."

At home, it wasn't so rosy. Although Barack Sr. hadn't seen his son in years, he ruled as a cruel disciplinarian. One evening, when Barry hoped to watch *Dr. Seuss' How the Grinch Stole Christmas!*—a holiday tradition in the Dunham household—his father ordered him to do his homework instead. "I tell you, Barry, you do not work as hard as you should," he scolded. "Go now, before I get angry at you." For Christmas, Barack Sr. gifted his son with his very first basketball, but the chill of their relationship never warmed. "It was only during the course of that month—by the end of that month—that I think I started to open myself up to understanding who he was," the future president later described. "But then he was gone, and I never saw him again." In 1982, 46-year-old Barack Sr. was killed in an automobile accident in Kenya.

"Your brains, your character," Ann told her son, "you got from your father."

Obama called his grandfather (here together in 1963) "Gramps" and his grandmother "Toot."

"HE FELT ABANDONED—HE FELT THAT HIS FATHER ABANDONED HIM AND HIS MOTHER WAS ALWAYS PURSUING HER CAREER."

—KEITH "RAY" KAKUGAWA, OBAMA'S HIGH SCHOOL FRIEND

Before living with his grandparents (seen here in 1941), Obama spent four years in Indonesia with his mother, Ann; stepfather, Lolo; and half-sister, Maya (below right).

But any joy that came from Barack Jr.'s birth was fleeting for the new maternal grandparents, because just weeks later, Ann packed up her newborn and moved back to Seattle to attend the University of Washington, her original first choice, without Barack Sr. Once there, the young mother juggled two evening courses—anthropology and political science—and her baby with help from her close girlfriends, who looked after him while she was in class. In March 1962, when Barack Jr. was just 7 months old, Ann upped her course load to three regular daytime classes. But although she received good marks, she wasn't feeling particularly accomplished. "I recall her being melancholy," remembered her high school friend Barbara Cannon Rusk. "I had a sense that something wasn't right in her marriage. It was all very mysterious. I didn't ask her about the relationship."

Back in Honolulu, Barack Sr. wasn't sharing much about his personal life with others either. Only one of his friends even knew that Ann, who was still legally his wife, or Barack Jr. existed. "For any of us to say that we knew Obama well would be difficult," fellow student Robert Ruenitz later explained. "He was a private man with academic achievement his foremost goal." Sure enough, when he graduated in June 1962, the *Honolulu Star-Bulletin* reported on the straight-A economics major who was headed to Harvard to get his PhD. "He plans to return to Africa and work in development of underdeveloped areas and international trade at the planning and policy-making level," explained the article. Years later, when Barack Jr. was in high school, he discovered the newspaper clipping folded up

amongst his birth certificate and old vaccination forms. "No mention is made of my mother or me," he wrote in his 1995 memoir, *Dreams From My Father*, of the moment he read the article for the first time. "I'm left to wonder whether the omission was intentional on my father's part, in anticipation of his long departure. Perhaps the reporter failed to ask personal questions, intimidated by my father's imperious manner; or perhaps it was an editorial decision, not part of the simple story that they were looking for. I wonder too whether the omission caused a fight between my parents."

By Ann's account, her estranged husband did ask her to come to the East Coast with him while he studied at Harvard, but she declined. "She had loved him," explained Barack Sr.'s eldest daughter, Auma Obama, who grew up in Kenya and met Ann decades later, "but she had feared having to give up too much of herself." Instead, she and Barack Jr. went back to Honolulu, where she returned to her previous life: She enrolled at the University of Hawaii again and moved in with her parents. But this time around, the family dynamic was a supportive one. As Madelyn worked at a local bank and Ann was immersed in her studies, Stanley, who was a young grandfather at only 45, spent his days looking after young Barack—or Barry, as they called him. Neil Abercrombie, the only friend of Barack Sr.'s who knew about the child, often saw the duo around the university campus. "Stanley loved that little boy," he recalled. "He took him everywhere.... In the absence of his father, there was not a kinder, more understanding man than Stanley Dunham. He was loving and generous."

But Barry's idyllic early days in Hawaii—which were made up of snorkeling and spearfishing with Gramps, neighborhood luaus and the island's famous shaved ices—would soon come to a halt. At the university, history repeated itself for Ann: That first semester back on campus in September 1962, the 19-year-old met and fell in love with Lolo (Martodihardjo) Soetoro, a 27-year-old Indonesian student who was working toward his graduate degree in geography. In January 1964, Ann filed for divorce from Barack Sr., citing "grievous mental suffering," and in March 1965, she and Lolo married, again without her friends or family present. Just a little more than a year later, her second husband was forced to return to his native Jakarta when the new military government there summoned all Indonesian students studying abroad, leaving behind his wife and stepson. Finally, in October 1967, after a year apart, Ann moved to Jakarta to be with Lolo, bringing along 6-year-old Barry.

Although exotic, his new home was a far cry from the life he enjoyed in Hawaii. Instead of the cozy two-bedroom apartment he'd shared with his grandparents, now Barry was residing in a small, flat-roofed bungalow with no electricity or plumbing, situated on a dirt road surrounded by wild birds, dogs, chickens and baby crocodiles. Viewed as a foreigner, it wasn't easy for him to make friends. The kids also teased Barry, who took his stepfather's surname, for being pudgy and nicknamed him Fatty. But as the years went by, he flourished. His first-grade teacher, Israella Darmawan, recalled him as one of her brightest students, "especially at mathematics," and he displayed his leadership skills even at a young age. "He always wanted to be No. 1, to be at the front." Barry also had bigger dreams at that time. When Darmawan asked him to write an essay on "What I Want to Be When I Grow Up," he wrote, "I will become president" —although it was unclear if he meant of Indonesia or his native United States.

It took young Barry just a year to master the Indonesian language, but his mother was adamant that he not lose his American identity or values. Each morning, before she went off to her job at the American embassy, Ann would drill her

"IF HIS FRIENDS WERE HAVING ARGUMENTS, HE'D BECOME A MEDIATOR. HE WOULD GRAB ONE FRIEND'S HAND AND GRAB THE OTHER FRIEND'S HAND AND FORCE THEM TO SHAKE."

—HARMON ASKIAR, CHILDHOOD PAL

son with lessons from an English correspondence course. "She would be totally exhausted," he recalled. "But it was very important to her that I never lose sight of who I was and where I fit in the scheme of things." During this time, Ann also made it a point to reinforce her son's black heritage, even though he had no relationship with his father, and had him read up on civil rights leaders like Martin Luther King Jr. and listen to the music of Sam Cooke, Aretha Franklin and Stevie Wonder.

But just as Barry was settling into life in Jakarta, Ann disrupted her son's harmony and sent him back to Hawaii to live with his grandparents to receive a better education in America. Stanley was able to pull some strings with his employer, an alumnus of the elite Punahou prep school, and ensure his grandson was accepted for the fifth grade. In August 1971, Ann—along with Barry's year-old half sister, Maya—tearfully said goodbye to the 10-year-old at the airport, sending him on his way to travel the 6,700 miles to Honolulu by himself. Impressively resilient, the young boy didn't let his circumstances get in the way of his studies—and he once again flourished at his new school. "Barry could whip out a paper that was due the next day the night before," remembered Suzanne Maurer, whose son Darin was one of his classmates. "The other kids spent weeks writing the same paper."

He also shed his extra weight and joined the basketball team.

Obama's sixth-grade teacher, Betty Morioka, described the boy (here on a class trip in 1972) as "charming."

Madelyn and Stanley Dunham were so special to their grandson (seen here at his high school graduation in 1979), one of his first words was *toot*—short for *tutu*, the Hawaiian word for grandparent.

Obama played on Punahou School's basketball team, which won the state championship in 1979.

and joined the basketball team. Although he wasn't a star player, he loved the game, even off the court. Bobby Titcomb, one of his close friends, recalled seeing Barry "dribbling his ball, running down the sidewalk on Punahou Street to his apartment, passing the ball between his legs. I mean, he was into it." Barry and Bobby also spent their free time enjoying all that nature had to offer. "We'd go hike up Peacock Flats and camp, just the two of us," said Titcomb. "We'd try to get away from everything.... And we'd talk about how the world could be."

"WE WERE POTHEADS. WE LOVED OUR BEER. WE LOVED BASKETBALL SO MUCH THAT WE COULDN'T GET ENOUGH OF IT. FOR US, IT WAS JUST ALL FUN AND GAMES AND BASKETBALL AND HANGING OUT, LISTENING TO MUSIC AND GOING TO THE BEACH."

—Tom Topolinski, Obama's high school friend

In 1972, after a year apart from her son, Ann left Lolo and returned yet again to Honolulu. She soon found a small apartment for her and her two children near the University of Hawaii, where she was pursuing a master's degree in anthropology. Finally, Barry got to live under the same roof as his mother and the baby sister he'd barely gotten to know before he was sent away. But that, too, was short-lived.

Just after Barry's 14th birthday, in 1975, Ann revealed she was returning to Indonesia to do fieldwork for her PhD—and it was up to him if he wanted to join her or stay in Hawaii. He made the decision to finish high school at Punahou, but it wasn't an easy one. "His biggest struggles were his feelings of abandonment," revealed his friend Keith "Ray" Kakugawa. Barry was also grappling with being biracial. "I began to think that as a black man being raised by white people, I should belong to both worlds," he later explained, "and yet I couldn't help feeling that I really belonged to neither."

The teen coped with his emotional scars the best way he could—with drugs and alcohol. "Junkie. Pothead. That's where I'd been headed: the final, fatal role of the young would-be black man," he acknowledged in *Dreams From My Father*. "Except the highs hadn't been about that, me trying to prove what a down brother I was.... I got high for just the opposite effect, something that could push questions of who I was out of my mind, something that could flatten out the landscape of my heart, blur the edges of my memory." Young Barry's behavior wasn't lost on his grandmother. "I had a few hints," she later admitted, "and I think I talked to him a little about it. But it didn't seem overwhelming or prolonged."

It also concerned his mother. Just before his senior year, Ann expressed her worry. "Don't you think you're being a little casual about your future?" she asked, he recalled. Barry played dumb. "What do you mean?" "You know exactly what I mean," she said. "One of your friends was just arrested for drug possession. Your grades are slipping. You haven't even started on your college applications. Whenever I try to talk to you about it, you act like I'm just this great big bother.... Damn it, Bar, you can't just sit around like some good-time Charlie, waiting for luck to see you through."

Her words were heard loud and clear by Barry, who graduated from Punahou in June 1979, his mother and grandparents cheering him on as he received his diploma. "Her worst fears hadn't come to pass," he wrote in 1995. "I had graduated without mishap, was accepted into several respectable schools and settled on Occidental College in Los Angeles, mainly because I'd met a girl from Brentwood while she was vacationing in Hawaii with her family. But I was still just going through the motions, as indifferent toward college as toward most everything else."

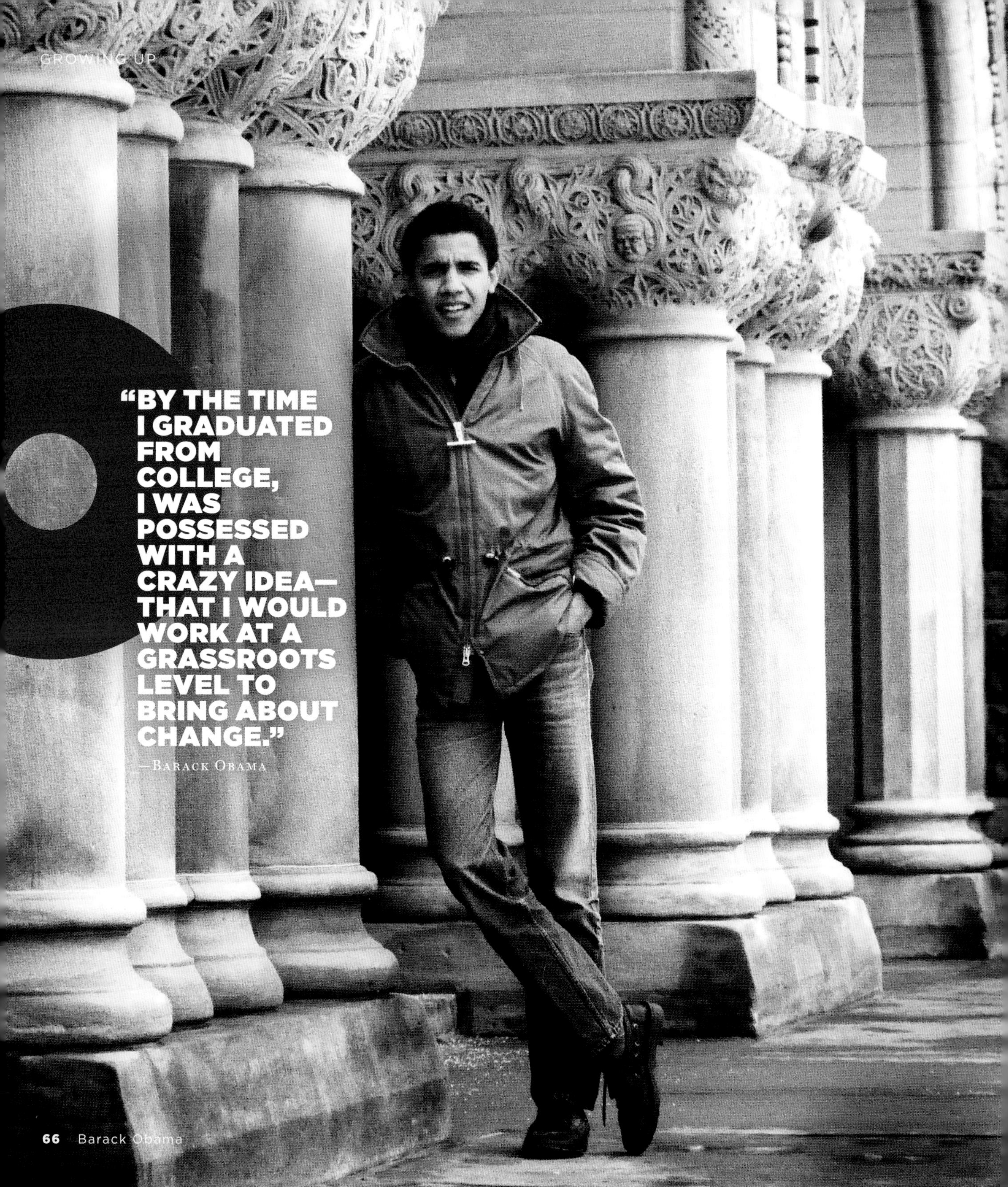

"BY THE TIME I GRADUATED FROM COLLEGE, I WAS POSSESSED WITH A CRAZY IDEA—THAT I WOULD WORK AT A GRASSROOTS LEVEL TO BRING ABOUT CHANGE."

—Barack Obama

HOW COLLEGE CHANGED HIM

AFTER TWO YEARS AT OCCIDENTAL COLLEGE, OBAMA TRANSFERRED TO COLUMBIA UNIVERSITY—WHERE HE MAJORED IN POLITICAL SCIENCE—BEFORE EARNING A LAW DEGREE AT HARVARD.

If Barack Obama's childhood and teen years were tarnished by disappointment and abandonment, once in college, he had the chance for a new start. In September 1979, the 18-year-old arrived at Occidental, a private liberal arts college in Los Angeles, and moved into room A104 in Haines Hall Annex. Although his native Hawaii was 2,500 miles away, Obama held onto the island's vibe, often wearing Hawaiian shirts, flip-flops, board shorts and a puka-shell necklace. His friend Eric Moore described him as "a definite surfer type" who, due to spending years in Indonesia, was "more worldly than the average kid in California.... But he still wanted to fit in."

And he did. Obama played a number of intramural sports, including tennis, flag football and water polo (surprisingly, he didn't make the basketball team, despite winning the state championship in high school). His freshman roommate Paul Carpenter recalled Obama being "an athletic guy" but also "super bright. He could get through the course work in a fraction of the time it took me." But just as he did back in Honolulu, the teen balanced all his hard work with plenty of play. His dorm room was known as party central, and many weekends were spent drinking until the sun rose on Monday morning and classes resumed.

Still, there was a pivotal change in Obama at Occidental. During his sophomore year, he made his public-speaking debut at a Black Student Alliance demonstration, demanding the college separate itself from its interests in apartheid South Africa. Although his oration lasted just two minutes, the future president commanded the attention of the lunchtime crowd of a few hundred who gathered to listen. In his 1995 memoir, *Dreams From My Father*, Obama relived the crucial moment.

"A couple of students were throwing a Frisbee on the lawn; others were standing off to the side, ready to break off to the library at any moment," he wrote. "Without waiting for a cue, I stepped up to the microphone. 'There's a struggle going on,' I said. My voice barely carried beyond the first few rows. A few people looked up, and I waited for the crowd to quiet. 'I say, there's a struggle going on!' The Frisbee players stopped. 'It's happening an ocean away. But it's a struggle that touches each and every one of us. Whether we know it or not. Whether we want it or not. A struggle that demands we choose sides. Not between black and white. Not between rich and poor. No—it's a harder choice than that. It's a choice between dignity and servitude. Between fairness and injustice. Between commitment and indifference. A choice between right and wrong...' I stopped. The crowd was quiet now, watching me. Somebody started to clap. 'Go on with it, Barack,' somebody else shouted. 'Tell it like it is.' Then the others started in, clapping, cheering, and I knew that I had them, that the connection had been made."

But just as Obama was hitting his stride at Occidental, after two years there, he longed for a change. Where would he go? He had learned that the college offered a transfer program with Columbia University in New York City, so he signed up. Although he was eager for the move east, the friends he had made at Occidental didn't want to see him go. "I think there was a lot of stuff going on in me," he later reasoned. "I was starting to work it through. It's hard to remake yourself around people who have known you for a long time." Obama had learned a friend would soon be vacating her apartment in Manhattan's Spanish Harlem neighborhood, near Columbia's campus, so he arranged to take it over from her. But when he showed up at the address on 109th Street, no one answered. "I spent my first night in Manhattan curled up in an alleyway," he recalled. He eventually moved into the apartment, but when he discovered it didn't have heat (or hot water), he quickly found a new place, a sixth-floor walkup on East 94th Street, with a friend from Los Angeles, Sohale "Hal" Siddiqi. The two shared a dark, cramped one-bedroom, sleeping on mattresses on the floor because they were so broke.

Along with his new city and new college, Obama also took on a new moniker: Barack. Why lose his Barry nickname after 19 years? "It was much more of an assertion that I was coming of age," he later explained. "An assertion of being comfortable with the fact that I was different and that I didn't need to try to fit in, in a certain way." There were plenty of other changes to Obama's life: He gave up alcohol, became a vegetarian and transformed his surfer style to turtlenecks and Levi's. Every morning before class, he'd get up early and run 3 miles. He spent his evenings either reading or writing in his journal or wandering around the city.

There was also a big secret he was keeping from his close friends. He was having an affair with a wealthy white woman, whom he described as having "dark hair, specks of green in her eyes. Her voice sounded like a wind chime." But the interracial relationship could never work. While visiting her stately country home, the two went to see a play by a young black playwright, and the audience was mostly black, with everybody "laughing and clapping and hollering like they were in church." Afterward, Obama's friend asked why black people

Obama's grandparents Stanley and Madelyn Dunham visited him in 1983 while he was at Columbia University in New York City.

were "so angry all the time," according to his memoir. The juxtaposition bothered him. She couldn't be black," he wrote. "She would if she could, but she couldn't. She could only be herself, and wasn't that enough?"

It was during this time, in spring 1983, following his graduation from Columbia with a bachelor's degree in political science, that Obama embraced his African side more deeply. Wanting to be a community organizer, he reached out to black politicians, civil rights organizations and community action groups to offer his support—but not one replied to his letters. In the meantime, he needed a paycheck, so he took a job as a research associate at Business International Corporation (BIC), a small publisher of newsletters. Within a few months, he was promoted to financial writer and given a substantial raise; but after a year on the job, he moved on to Ralph Nader's New York Public Interest Research Group as a community organizer, working out of its Harlem campus. That position too grew stale, and Obama began eyeing his next step.

In the summer of 1985, he came upon a job listing looking for a community organizer trainee—in Chicago. Eager to make another big move, Obama sent in his résumé—and before he knew it, the man who'd placed the ad, Jerry Kellman, called him for a two-hour phone interview. "He was clearly very bright," recalled Kellman. "But there are a lot of very bright young people out there. But he was also mature, confident, articulate." A week later, the two met face-to-face at an Upper East Side coffee shop. Kellman, a Jew, had been attempting in vain to convince powerful black churches in Chicago to help him battle against the city's growing unemployment among its urban class; but no one took him seriously, since there weren't any African Americans on his staff. "I can't break through," he explained to Obama, whom he'd originally assumed was Japanese, based on his last name. "So that's why I need someone like you." Although the pay wasn't great—$10,000, less than a quarter of what he had been making at BIC—Obama took the job on the spot, because it was exactly what he was looking for.

But he had to work twice as hard to make it worthwhile. Every 12-hour day was spent making at least 30 phone calls from the cramped office of the

"WHAT BARACK REALLY WANTED WAS TO BE A CIVIL RIGHTS ORGANIZER... AND THIS WAS THE CLOSEST THING HE COULD FIND."

—Jerry Kellman, Obama mentor

grassroots Developing Communities Project (DCP) at Holy Rosary Church. Although 24-year-old Obama was a hit with older black women, who called him "Baby Face" and wanted to introduce him to their daughters, pastors made no time for the young do-gooder, which he found incredibly discouraging. While at DCP, he did enjoy a few successes—most significantly, crusading to remove asbestos from Altgeld Gardens, a decaying public housing project—but after two-and-a-half years, Obama felt his hands were tied when it came to bringing greater reform. "I'm not going to accomplish anything significant," he told his close confidant, local black leader Reverend Jeremiah Wright, "unless I get a law degree." With his eye on Harvard, Obama enlisted several influential figures, including Black Panther Party mentor Khalid Abdullah Tariq al-Mansour and Northwestern University professor John McKnight, to help him get accepted into the Ivy League institution that counted former presidents Teddy Roosevelt, Franklin Roosevelt and John F. Kennedy amongst its alumni. In February 1988, Obama received the response he was hoping for—he had been accepted into the university's prestigious law school.

At Harvard, Obama wasted no time getting down to business. The 27-year-old spent long hours in the school's library studying case law and statutes late into the night. His work ethic was particularly impressive to Larry Tribe, one of Harvard's best-known constitutional scholars, who brought Obama on as his research assistant to help with two books he was writing, *On Reading the Constitution* and *Abortion: The Clash of*

Before Obama became president of the Harvard Law Review, he worked as its editor his first year.

Absolutes. "Barack didn't come to an issue with a set of prepackaged ideas," explained Tribe. "He was entirely open to new approaches, fresh ways of looking at things. Back then, when he was just a first-year law student, I didn't hesitate to tell people that he was amazing—the most all-around impressive student I'd seen in decades."

Obama also made history during his second year at Harvard. In February 1990, he was elected president of the Harvard Law Review, the first time ever for an African American. The honor came with a wave of national media attention, and he was featured in *The New York Times*, the *Los Angeles Times*, the Associated Press and *Time* magazine, as well as TV interviews.

As a result of Obama's time in the spotlight, he was pursued by multiple publishers, all offering him a book deal to tell his extraordinary story. In the end, he settled on Poseidon Press, a small imprint of Simon & Schuster, and received a $150,000 advance. "I, imagining myself to have something original to say about the current state of race relations, agreed to take off a year after graduation and put my thoughts to paper," he wrote in *Dreams From My Father*, which would become his first of many memoirs. (Obama struggled for years to meet deadlines, and the book was eventually published in 1995.)

Despite his newfound fame, Obama was determined not to get distracted from his original post-Harvard plan. In an interview with *The Boston Globe*, he vowed he would return to Chicago after graduation because "I have a certain mission to make sure that the gifts I've received are plowed back into the community." Indeed, every summer during his three years at the Massachusetts university, he went back to the Windy City, where he gained valuable experience working at law firms. And when he graduated magna cum laude in 1991, Obama made good on his promise to make it his official home. In debt by $60,000 because of school loans, Obama sold almost everything in his apartment to fund his move. Any leftover personal items were then loaded into his mustard-yellow Toyota Tercel, bound for the next chapter. "I went into Harvard with a certain set of values," he later recounted. "I promised myself that I would leave Harvard with those same values. And I did." ○

"WE ALL HAVE A RESPONSIBILITY TO USE OUR LEGAL TRAINING IN WAYS THAT MAKE THIS COUNTRY WORK BETTER."

—Barack Obama, in his Harvard Law yearbook

Pilgrimage to Kenya

Following the death of Barack Obama Sr. in Nairobi, Kenya, in 1982, Barack Jr. was inspired to visit his homeland and learn more about the father he never knew. In the summer of 1988, before he began Harvard Law School, the 27-year-old set out to retrace his roots, beginning with three weeks spent in his maternal side's native England and Scotland. "It wasn't that Europe wasn't beautiful," he later said. "It just wasn't mine." But once Obama stepped foot in Kenya, he finally found what was his. For five weeks, he absorbed all he could about his father from the relatives he had never met before, including Barack Sr.'s first wife, Kezia; five half-brothers; two half-sisters; a step-grandmother; and countless more uncles, aunts and cousins—an overwhelming experience that he said left him feeling "exhausted and numb."

But the defining moment of his pilgrimage was when Obama stood in front of his father's unmarked grave in the yard of the tin-roof home he'd shared with his third wife, Sarah. The 46-year-old Barack Sr., who had lost both of his legs in a previous drunken car accident, had been driving himself home after a night of revelry when he crashed his car into a 6-foot-high tree stump and was killed instantly.

It wasn't until the end of his trip, when Obama's older half-sister, Auma, brought him to Mombasa, Kenya's second-largest city, that it evolved into something "magical," he later explained. After immersing himself in his estranged father's past, he felt "much more forgiving of him."

Obama again visited his relatives in Kenya in 1987.

MEETING MICHELLE

IN THE SUMMER OF 1989, OBAMA'S LIFE WAS FOREVER CHANGED WHEN MICHELLE ROBINSON WAS ASSIGNED TO BE HIS MENTOR AT A CHICAGO LAW FIRM.

"I REMEMBER HOW, THE FIRST TIME I TOOK HER BACK TO HAWAII, GRAMPS NUDGED MY RIBS AND SAID MICHELLE WAS QUITE 'A LOOKER.'"

—Barack Obama, on bringing Michelle home for Christmas 1989

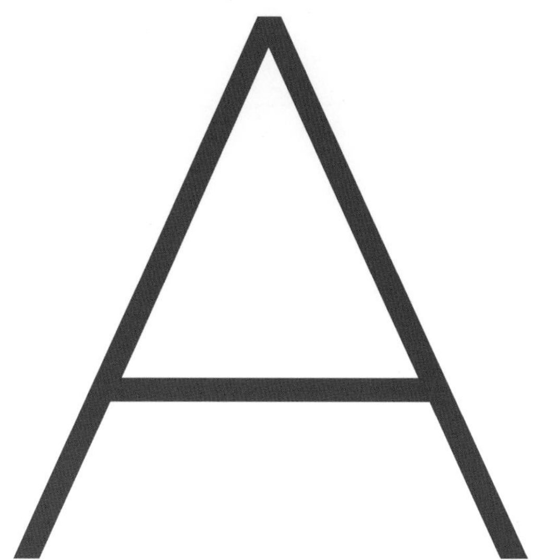

After graduating from Harvard Law School in May 1991, Barack Obama headed to Chicago to fulfill his dream of being a community organizer. Little did he know what the city would give him in return: the greatest love of his life. Two years earlier, he had interviewed for a summer job at the Midwest office of the Sidley Austin law firm, where he was supposed to meet with a trio of lawyers, including Michelle Robinson. But as fate would have it, she was too busy that day to vet the candidate, so she asked her colleague Joe Levi to handle it in her place. "I was wowed by Barack," Levi recalled years later. "I thought he was phenomenal. He was one of the best interviews I've ever had, really.... I called Michelle later in the day and said, 'Boy, did you miss a good one'"—to which she replied, "That's what everybody is telling me."

Obama may have missed meeting Michelle during the interview process, but once he got the job, she was selected to be his mentor because of their Harvard ties (she'd graduated in 1988 with a law degree). Before he started, Michelle called to go over what he could expect. "She was very corporate and very proper on the phone," he later revealed, "trying to explain to me how the summer program at Sidley Austin was going to go." And when he showed up on his first day in June 1989—albeit slightly late due to the rain—one could argue that it was love at first sight the moment he walked into her office. "He was actually cute and a lot more articulate and impressive than I expected," Michelle revealed in 2004. "My first job was to take him to lunch, and we ended up talking for what seemed like hours." Although she found him to have "a good sense of humor," she was put off by the fact "he had this bad sport jacket and a cigarette dangling from his mouth."

Likewise, the 28-year-old law student was taken by the Chicago native three years his junior. "He came in one day and said, 'My mentor is really hot,'" remembered Sidley's Rob Fisher. And Obama made it pretty clear to Michelle how he felt, added another colleague, Kelly Jo MacArthur. "He would try to charm her, flirt with her, and she would act very professional. He was undeniably charming and interesting and attractive," yet Michelle kept refusing his nearly daily requests to go out on a date, on the basis it would be improper as his adviser. "That's a poor excuse," he recalled telling her. "Come on, what advice are you giving me? You're showing me how the copy machine works." Obama even offered to quit Sidley for a chance with Michelle. Still, she turned him down—and even tried to set him up with several of her girlfriends. But he wouldn't take no for an answer, and weeks later, Michelle finally agreed to go out with Obama on one condition: "We won't call it a date. I will spend the day with you." On June 30, the two went on their lunch break together to the Art Institute of Chicago, a few blocks from their office. "He was talking Picasso," Michelle recalled. "He impressed me with his knowledge of art...and we talked and we talked."

Their first "nondate" was so special, Obama didn't want it to end. He suggested they get together again that evening to go to the movies and see Spike Lee's *Do the Right Thing*. At the theater, Michelle's biggest fear came true when they ran into Sidley colleague Newton Minor and his wife, who could tell "they were a little embarrassed" to be seen together. Still, Obama and Michelle's evening continued with drinks on the roof of the John Hancock Building.

Despite her concern with becoming fodder for office gossip, Michelle was too intrigued by Obama to end

After meeting Michelle, Obama's mother bragged to a friend, "She is intelligent.... She did her BA at Princeton and her law degree at Harvard."

"OH, MICHELLE WAS FULL OF PLANS, ON THE FAST TRACK, WITH NO TIME, SHE TOLD ME, FOR DISTRACTIONS—ESPECIALLY MEN."

—Barack Obama, on his first conversation with Michelle

things. For their second date, she accompanied him to one of his Developing Communities Project training sessions with single mothers at a local church, where she saw a different side of him. "I knew then and there, there's obviously something different about this guy," she later said. "It touched me.... He made me think in ways that I hadn't before. What I saw in him on that day was authenticity and truth and principle. That's who I fell in love with...that's why I fell in love with him."

A few days later, Obama and Michelle had their first kiss during an ice cream date at Baskin-Robbins, just a few blocks from the home she shared with her parents (according to Obama, their lip-lock "tasted like chocolate"). From that moment, the couple were inseparable, as they tried to spend as much time together before he headed back to Harvard for his fall semester. In late July, Michelle introduced her new boyfriend to her parents, Fraser and Marian Robinson, and her older brother, Craig. The trio was easily impressed with the "smart, easygoing" guy, but Craig didn't allow himself to get too attached, given his sister's history of breaking hearts. "Too bad he won't be around for long," he thought to himself. So he was surprised when, a few weeks later, Michelle asked him to take Obama to play basketball, since "you can tell a lot about a personality on the court." Craig, a former Princeton basketball star who had been drafted into the NBA, determined that Obama had passed the test. "This guy is first-rate," he reported back to Michelle, noting that he was "very team-oriented, very unselfish" with the ball.

Just as the romance was heating up, it was time for Obama to head back to Harvard for his second year. Over the next few months, he and Michelle traveled thousands of miles between Chicago and Cambridge to see each other. "We were both determined," he recalled, "to do whatever it took to make it work." After celebrating Thanksgiving with the Robinsons, Michelle joined Obama in Honolulu to spend Christmas with his family—and that's when talk of marriage first came up. In a letter Obama's mother, Ann Dunham, sent to a friend, she gushed about her son's girlfriend and gave her stamp of approval. "If he goes ahead and marries her after he finishes law school," she wrote, "I will have no objections."

Over the next two years, Obama and Michelle worked hard to keep a long-distance relationship alive, with him in Cambridge and her in Chicago. But when she brought up the topic of marriage, he'd dismiss it. "The issue had become a bone of contention between us," she later acknowledged. And it was one that she addressed yet again in July 1991 during a dinner date to celebrate his passing the bar exam. "Marriage, it doesn't mean anything," Obama insisted. "We know we love

Michelle was "deeply moved" when Obama took her to Kenya to meet his family in 1992.

The Woman Who Turned Him Down

Before Michelle, another woman almost became Mrs. Obama. Beginning in the mid-1980s, Obama was involved with anthropologist Sheila Miyoshi Jager, who was also biracial. The two moved in together after meeting while doing community organizing in Chicago. Soon enough, Obama wanted to marry her. Twice he proposed, and twice she declined.

The first time was in 1986, during a visit with her parents, who thought their 23-year-old was too young. Obama and Jager remained together three more years, until he left for Harvard. Before he moved, he proposed again—"Out of a sense of desperation over our eventual parting and not in any real faith in our future," she recalled—and Jager reasoned she had to travel to Korea for dissertation research.

But their love remained—even after Obama began a relationship with Michelle. In early 1990, Jager took a teaching fellowship at Harvard—and Obama juggled both women. "I always felt bad about it," she confessed in David J. Garrow's 2017 Obama biography, *Rising Star*. In 1991, she ended it when she fell for another man. "As much as I loved him, I was relieved when our paths finally parted," Jager explained. "We went through many painful things together."

The "Obama Kissing Rock," in Chicago's Hyde Park, commemorates the spot where Obama and Michelle shared their first kiss, in July 1989.

"IT WAS MAGICAL. THEY WERE CLEARLY MADLY IN LOVE WITH EACH OTHER."

—Valerie Jarrett, family friend, on Barack and Michelle Obama's wedding day

Barack Obama

Michelle and Obama—with their mothers, Marian Robinson and Ann Dunham—on their wedding day.

each other. What do we need to get married for?" His words incensed Michelle, who went on a tirade that continued even as the waiter arrived with their dessert. "I'm not one of these girls who'll just hang out forever," she told him. "That's just not who I am." But when she looked down at her plate and saw a small velvet box, she was rendered speechless: Inside was a 1-carat diamond ring. As Obama slipped it onto her finger, he joked, "That kind of shuts you up, doesn't it?"

Less than a year later, on October 3, 1992, Obama and Michelle exchanged vows in front of 130 of their closest friends and family at Chicago's Trinity United Church of Christ. The groom's mentor, Jeremiah Wright, who'd helped him get into Harvard, officiated the ceremony, and the bride's maid of honor, Santita Jackson, sang as she walked down the aisle. At their reception at the South Shore Cultural Center, which had once been an exclusive whites-only country club, the couple shared their first dance as husband and wife to Stevie Wonder's "You and I." For their two-week honeymoon, they drove up the coast of California along the Pacific Coast Highway, from Santa Barbara to San Francisco. "Putting the two of them together was like putting hydrogen and oxygen together to create this unbelievable life force," described their friend Kelly Jo MacArthur. "We understood that together they were going to be so much more than they would have been individually."

Once back in Chicago, the newlyweds lived with Michelle's mother (her father had died in 1991) as they searched for their perfect first home, a $277,500 four-bedroom condo near Hyde Park, where they'd shared their first kiss three years earlier. The young couple was so broke—their combined monthly student loans were more than their mortgage payment—Obama's grandmother gifted them most of the $111,000 down payment.

Starting a family was always the plan for Obama and Michelle. But as he focused on building his career, the couple struggled to make that dream a reality, since work kept him from the home Monday through Friday. Seeing her husband only on weekends was tough, revealed mutual Obama friend Valerie Jarrett. "Michelle was feeling lonely, desperately so." And after four years of unsuccessfully trying to conceive, the couple were considering adoption—until a home pregnancy test confirmed they were finally going to be parents.

On July 4, 1998, their daughter Malia Ann was born—and bonded Obama and Michelle deeply. With Dad a night owl and Mom an early bird, the two were the perfect team as they split baby duties. "While Michelle got some well-earned sleep, I would stay up until one or two in the morning," he explained, "changing diapers, heating breast milk, feeling my daughter's soft breath against my chest as I rocked her to sleep, guessing at her infant dreams."

Nearly three years later, on June 10, 2001, the Obamas made Malia a big sister with the birth of their second daughter, Natasha Marian, whom they called Sasha. "By the time Sasha was born—just as beautiful, and almost as calm as her sister—my wife's anger toward me seemed barely contained," revealed Obama, whose career was once again keeping him away from home for extended periods. "'You only think about yourself,' she would tell me. 'I never thought I'd have to raise a family alone.'" But when the newborn battled meningitis that September, the terrified parents grew closer than they'd ever been. Five years later, in his 2006 memoir *The Audacity of Hope*, Obama sang Michelle's praises as a wife and mother and acknowledged her sacrifices for their family.

"For no matter how liberated I liked to see myself as—no matter how much I told myself that Michelle and I were equal partners and that her dreams and ambitions were as important as my own—the fact was that when children showed up, it was Michelle and not I who was expected to make the necessary adjustments," he wrote in his second book. "Sure, I helped, but it was always on my terms, on my schedule. Meanwhile, she was the one who had to put her career on hold. She was the one who had to make sure that the kids were fed and bathed every night. If Malia or Sasha got sick or the babysitter failed to show up, it was she who, more often than not, had to get on the phone to cancel a meeting at work.... In the end, I credit Michelle's strength—her willingness to manage these tensions and make sacrifices on behalf of myself and the girls—with carrying us through the difficult times." ●

In 2004, the Obamas brought along Malia and Sasha when they voted for him for the U.S. Senate.

FROM Lawyer TO Senator

FOLLOWING HARVARD, OBAMA WORKED AS A LAWYER AND COLLEGE PROFESSOR BEFORE BEING ELECTED TO THE ILLINOIS SENATE IN 1996—FOLLOWED BY THE U.S. SENATE EIGHT YEARS LATER.

“I remember thinking he had a snowball’s chance in hell,” Illinois politician Toni Preckwinkle said of Obama’s run for the U.S. Senate.

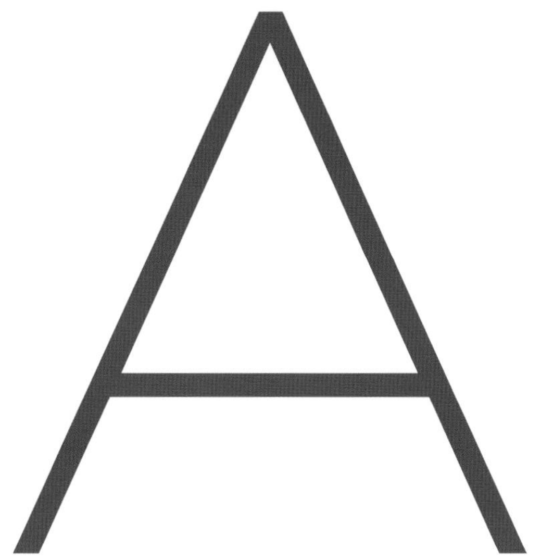

Although he'd earned a law degree from Harvard, Barack Obama always had bigger dreams for himself beyond the courtroom. "I thought I might like to get into politics," he revealed to Michelle's brother, Craig Robinson, not long after meeting him in 1989. "I was really thinking more on a national scale. Maybe run for Congress or the Senate. Who knows? If I did a good job, I might even run for president someday." "Don't say that too loud," his future brother-in-law jokingly warned. "Someone might hear you and think you were nuts."

Even before Obama's graduation from the Ivy League university in June 1991, potential employers were vying to land the hotshot who had been elected the first African American president of the Harvard Law Review. When Chicago attorney Judson Miner called Obama's Harvard campus office to offer him a job, his assistant explained, "You can leave your name and take a number. You're number six hundred and forty-seven." Obama could have had any legal job he wanted—he just didn't want any of them. He also turned down a position with Sidley Austin, the first law firm he worked for, in 1989, and where he'd met Michelle. "I think I'm going to go into politics," he explained to senior partner Newton Minow, who praised his decision. The 30-year-old also refused a proposal by U.S. Court of Appeals Judge Abner Mikva to be his clerk in Washington, D.C., in favor of entering politics in Chicago. "Boy, this guy has got more chutzpah than Dick Tracy," Mikva thought to himself. "Has he got something to learn. You don't just come to Chicago and plant your flag."

And that's exactly what Obama discovered. Once back in the Windy City, the graduate consulted with many of his powerful local friends, including civil rights activist and two-time presidential nominee candidate Jesse Jackson, whose daughter Santita was friends with Michelle. And what he learned was that Mayor Richard M. Daley held the key to political power in Illinois. But how would he get close to him? Obama devised a plan in which he persuaded Michelle, by then his fiancée, to submit her résumé to Daley, asking to join his staff. This woman is no longer interested in being at her law firm," a Daley staffer noted on Michelle's cover letter. "She wants to be in government and give back." Once the mayor's deputy chief of staff, Valerie Jarrett, received Michelle's résumé, she wasted no time calling her for an interview. "I was just unbelievably bowled over by how impressive she was," recalled Jarrett. "I offered [a job] to her on the spot, which was totally inappropriate, because I should have talked to the mayor first. But I just knew that she was really special."

There was just one thing holding Michelle back from accepting: The position as Daley's assistant paid only $60,000, half of what she had been earning as a lawyer. How would she and Obama be able to pay off their $300,000 in student loans and survive on such a meager salary? He convinced her they'd be able to make it work, but Michelle wasn't entirely sure she wanted to make the career move, revealed Jarrett: "She had some serious reservations about whether she was going to leave the practice of law and leap

Before a March 2004 televised debate with his U.S. Senate opponents, Obama studied notes in his Chicago campaign office.

into the mayor's office in a political environment." In the end, Michelle accepted the job—and with her new role, she was able to network with the city's powers that be and made contacts that benefited Obama, including leaders of the African American business community. After just a few months with Mayor Daley, Michelle's mentor Jarrett was picked to head Chicago's Department of Planning and Development, and she brought along the assistant as the city's new economic development coordinator—which gave her even greater access to the top tier of Chicago's business community.

As Obama figured out his next move, he accepted a position as a fellow in law and government at University of Chicago Law School, which he juggled with writing his manuscript for Simon & Schuster. Although then-law school dean Geoffrey Stone hoped Obama would come on full-time once he finished his first book, secretary Charlotte Maffia could see he was destined for more, telling her boss, "He's going to be governor of Illinois some day!" Until then, Obama dedicated his efforts to his first love, private service. He became a founding member of the nonprofit Public Allies, which signed up young people to provide services to the poor. Ahead of the 1992 election, he also directed the Project Vote campaign, which achieved its goal of registering 150,000 of 400,000 unregistered African Americans. As a result of Project Vote's accomplishment, Democratic presidential nominee Bill Clinton secured Illinois—the first time the state had gone blue since Lyndon Johnson was elected in 1964.

On the heels of that historic feat, more local leaders' doors opened for Obama, and he took full advantage of the valuable new connections. During this time, he met Bettylu Saltzman, daughter of Chicago shopping-mall magnate and former commerce secretary Philip M. Klutznick, who made a crucial introduction between the political hopeful and David Axelrod, chief political consultant to former Mayor Harold Washington and current Mayor Daley. "I think he was strategic in his choice of friends and mentors," Chicago alderman Toni Preckwinkle said of Obama. "I think he saw the positions he held as stepping-stones to other things." That was exactly his motive when he reached out to Judson Miner, the local attorney who'd previously been told he was 647th in line to offer the Harvard grad a job at his civil rights firm, Davis, Miner, Barnhill & Galland. Coincidentally, Miner was the city's chief lawyer and one of the masterminds behind Mayor Washington's rise to power—and now he had Obama's full attention. In 1993, the young lawyer joined his 13-attorney firm specializing in civil rights litigation and neighborhood economic development as an associate. (In 1996, Obama was

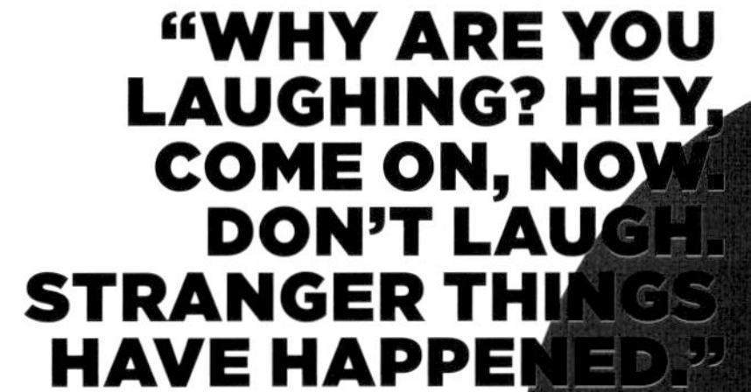

"WHY ARE YOU LAUGHING? HEY, COME ON, NOW. DON'T LAUGH. STRANGER THINGS HAVE HAPPENED."

— Barack Obama, to his wife, Michelle, when he shared his plans to run for the Senate and then the presidency

Obama (here in 1992) taught constitutional law at University of Chicago Law School for 12 years, until 2004.

promoted to counsel, where he remained, even as he worked in politics, until 2004.)

But with his sights set on becoming Chicago's next mayor, Obama wasn't keen on Michelle's association with Daley, who was unpopular with black voters. Lucky for him, she was growing weary of her job in City Hall and open to a new possibility. His suggestion? Executive director of Public Allies, the nonprofit he had founded. "It sounded risky and just out there," she later said. "But for some reason, it just spoke to me. This was the first time I said, 'This is what I say I care about. Right here. And I will have to run it.'" As Michelle, who by then was his wife, excelled in the role, Obama focused on his next move—and by now he was looking beyond local mayor. In August 1994, Congressman Mel Reynolds was indicted (and later, convicted) for having sex with an underage campaign worker and resigned from his position—which piqued the interest of Senator Alice Palmer. And if she vacated her seat for Reynolds' in Congress, that would pave the way for Obama to succeed her in the Senate.

At a July 1995 book party to celebrate the release of *Dreams From My Father* (below) in Chicago, the author's potential political move was a hot topic of conversation. But as one attendee remembers, Michelle was "clearly not enthusiastic," like everyone else, about the possibility of him working in the state's capital. "It's beneath you, Barack," she later told her husband. "It's too small-time. What can you possibly accomplish in Springfield?" Despite her reservations, in September the

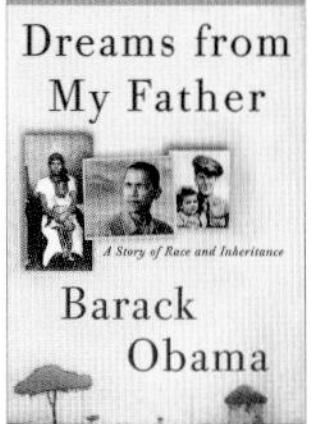

Democrat announced his run for Illinois State Senate to more than 200 supporters at the Ramada Inn Lakeshore in Hyde Park-Kenwood, the 13th District he hoped to represent. "Barack Obama carries on the tradition of independence in this district," Senator Palmer said when she introduced her potential successor. "His candidacy is a passing of the torch."

But as his political dream was closer to becoming a reality, Obama's personal life was about to be rocked by a devastating loss. His mother, Ann Dunham, had been diagnosed with uterine and ovarian cancer, and her prognosis wasn't good, although she insisted to her son she was doing fine and that he should focus on his campaign instead of coming to Hawaii to be with her. On November 7, with Obama still in Chicago, the 52-year-old lost her battle, and the guilt remains with her son. "The single greatest regret of my life," he would later confess, "was not being there when my mother died."

He was about to hit another roadblock. After Palmer was defeated in the primary, it was becoming evident she was not going to win Reynolds' spot in Congress. Local black leaders approached Obama about withdrawing from the Senate race and allowing the African American to reclaim her seat; he refused. But Palmer would not go down without a fight. On the deadline to get her name on the ballot for the March 1996 election, she provided 1,580 signatures from registered voters, twice the number required. Suspicious of how she'd pulled off such a feat, Obama ordered his campaign workers to take a closer look at the names on the petitions at the Chicago Board of Elections. What they uncovered was a wealth of irregularities, disqualifying two-thirds of Palmer's signatures and banning her from the ballot. Obama then carried out the same investigation with his other opponents and made a similar discovery. As a result, he ran unopposed and won. When the *Chicago*

For his U.S. Senate campaign in 2004, Obama managed to raise $10 million.

The Senator's Defining Moment

As Obama campaigned for U.S. Senator in 2004, the country got its first introduction to the young up-and-coming politician. He was selected to be the keynote speaker at the Democratic National Convention, a moment he knew would be a game changer. In the weeks leading up to it, Obama spent countless hours writing and revising his speech, with notes he received from presidential nominee Senator John Kerry's staff. Not only would this be the first time he appeared on national television or used a teleprompter, but it would also be the biggest crowd he had ever addressed (more than 5,000 were expected at Boston's Fleet Center, with millions more watching from home).

Before Obama even stepped onstage, he had the crowd of Democrats in the palm of his hand. His friend Marty Nesbitt described the senator's walk to the venue "like it was Tiger Woods at the Masters." And once there, his 17-minute speech didn't disappoint. Obama began with his story as the son of a Kenyan who "grew up herding goats" and a white mother from Kansas. As he pumped up Kerry and encouraged those watching to elect him, he electrified the delegates in attendance, who interrupted him 33 times with their cheers. Obama ended his speech with a message of "hope," a theme of his campaign. "The hope of a skinny kid with a funny name who believes America has a place for him too," he said of himself. "Hope! Hope in the face of difficulty! Hope in the face of uncertainty! The audacity of hope! In the end, that is God's greatest gift to us, the bedrock of this nation. A belief in things not seen. A belief that there are better days ahead."

Obama's speech not only inspired Democrats, it defined his future as one of the party's brightest stars, destined for the highest office. MSNBC's Chris Matthews called it that night on his broadcast. "I have to tell you, a little chill in my legs right now," he described. "That is an amazing moment in history right there. A keynoter like I have never heard.... I have seen the first black president there."

After Obama's DNC speech, Michelle worried that "things will never be normal again" for their family.

"BARACK HAS A FIRST-CLASS TEMPERAMENT AND A FIRST-CLASS INTELLECT. IT WAS A VERY, VERY, VERY LONG SHOT. BUT I TOLD HIM TO GO FOR IT."

—Attorney Newton Minow, on Obama's U.S. Senate run

In 2005, the U.S. senator threw out the first pitch in Game 2 of the American League Championship Series between the Chicago White Sox and the Los Angeles Angels.

Tribune accused him of denying voters the right to choose their candidate, he insisted, "I think they ended up with a very good state senator."

As impressive as his de facto win was for a political rookie, when he arrived in Springfield in January 1997, his reputation as a hotshot Harvard lawyer preceded him. "You don't belong here," accused Democrat Denny Jacobs. Complicating matters, Republicans controlled the Senate, making it nearly impossible to make much change—although he did have some wins. Obama brought reform to the death penalty system and co-sponsored a bill that restructured the Illinois welfare program, in addition to helping pass legislation that established a $100 million Earned Income Tax Credit for working families, as well as increased child-care subsidies for low-income families. Despite his efforts to aid the state's struggling citizens, the 36-year-old faced criticism from his fellow African American senators, especially those who represented urban areas. "What do you know, Barack?" accused Rickey Hendon during one of their many intense debates on the Senate floor. "You grew up in Hawaii, and you live in Hyde Park. What do you know about the street?" To which Obama replied, "I know a lot. I didn't exactly have a rosy childhood."

Due to that isolation, Obama turned to the mostly white legislators from the suburban and rural southern parts of Illinois, bonding on the golf course and at weekly poker games. "I learned, if you're willing to listen to people, it's possible to bridge a lot of the differences that dominate the national political debate," Obama later said. "I pretty quickly got to form relationships with Republicans...and we had a lot in common."

Obama was reelected to the Illinois Senate twice before he eyed his next step on his career path, the U.S. Senate, in 2002. But not only was he considered a long shot, friends warned his political aspirations were threatening his marriage. So when he revealed his plan to Michelle, he made her a promise. "I really think there is a strong possibility that I can win this race," he explained. "If you are willing to go with me on this ride, and if it doesn't work out, then I will step out of politics." Although she wasn't the biggest fan of his decision to run, Michelle supported her husband, even standing in for him at several fundraisers and rallies.

Time magazine called Obama "The political equivalent of a rainbow—a sudden preternatural event inspiring awe and ecstasy."

But she didn't let him out of his domestic duties. One Saturday morning, as he headed out to a candidates' forum, she insisted he bring along their daughters, Malia and Sasha. "You've been gone all week," she told him, "and I've got stuff to do today." At the meeting, Obama unsuccessfully juggled both jobs. Daniel Hynes, who ran against Obama, recalled feeling "a little sorry for the guy.... There he was, trying to herd these two little kids, and they're knocking things over and taking pamphlets and throwing them. And here he is, trying to be this dignified Senate candidate."

On November 2, 2004, all the sacrifices proved worth it when Obama easily defeated his Republican opponent, Alan Keyes, 70 percent to 27 percent—the largest margin for a statewide race in Illinois history.

The Obamas celebrated his 2004 election to the U.S. Senate in Chicago.

"HE KNOCKED OFF THE INCUMBENTS, SO THAT RIGHT THERE GAVE HIM SOME NOTORIETY. AND HE RAN UNOPPOSED—WHICH FOR A ROOKIE IS UNHEARD OF."

—PRECINCT COORDINATOR RON DAVIS, ON OBAMA'S 1996 SENATE WIN

But his success would once again come at a cost for his family. Although he wanted Michelle and the girls to move with him to Washington, D.C., she believed that remaining in Chicago–where she had a strong support system, including her mother, was the best decision. So the Senator rented a one-bedroom apartment near Georgetown Law School, where he stayed Tuesday through Thursday before flying to Chicago on Fridays for Saturday meetings—which often left just Sundays reserved for his family.

While away from his wife and daughters, Obama focused on his next political move. Although he had insisted he'd serve his six-year senatorial term and not run for president in 2008, by 2006 he had changed his mind. In late October, as his second book, *The Audacity of Hope*, climbed the best-seller charts, the buzz surrounding the popular politician reached a fever pitch. A week after he appeared on *The Oprah Winfrey Show*, *Time* magazine splashed him across its cover with the headline "Why Barack Obama Could Be the Next President." On October 22, he opened up about his plans to Tim Russert on NBC's *Meet the Press*, but stopped short of saying they were concrete. "I have not made a decision to pursue higher office, but it is true that I have thought about it over the last several months. I don't want to be coy about this... I have thought about the possibility, but I have not thought about it with the seriousness and depth that I think is required.... After November 7, I'll sit down, I'll sit down and consider, and if at some point I change my mind, I will make a public announcement—and everybody will be able to go at me."

Before accepting the presidential nomination "with profound gratitude and great humility" at the Democratic National Convention on August 28, 2008, Senator Obama had a quiet moment alone backstage.

FOR THE WHITE HOUSE

IN 2008, OBAMA MADE A HISTORIC RUN AGAINST SENATOR JOHN MCCAIN AND WAS ELECTED AMERICA'S FIRST AFRICAN AMERICAN PRESIDENT.

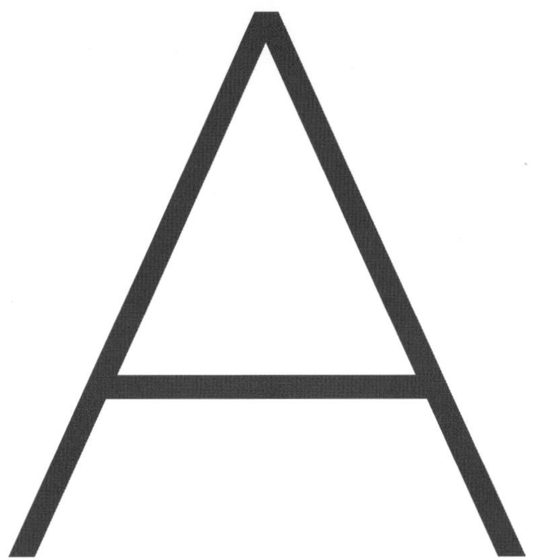

Although Barack Obama's mind was made up when it came to running for president of the United States in the 2008 election, convincing his wife was going to be his toughest sell. Not only was Michelle concerned about how the grueling campaign would affect their young family, but she was unsure that her husband, a relatively amateur politician with only a few years in the national spotlight, could beat former first lady Hillary Clinton in the Democratic primaries. According to Obama's chief strategist, David Axelrod, "She didn't want Barack to launch some kind of empty effort here." But by Christmas 2006, while vacationing in Hawaii, the U.S. senator from Illinois was finally able to change Michelle's mind. During a walk on the beach, "We just talked it through," he later revealed. "It wasn't as if it was a slam dunk for me."

Two months later, on February 10, 2007, Obama announced his candidacy as the Democratic nominee in front of 15,000 people gathered outside the Old State Capitol Building in Springfield, Illinois—the same place Abraham Lincoln gave his famous "House Divided" speech in 1858, before he was elected president. "I know I haven't spent a lot of time learning the ways of Washington. But I've been there long enough to know that the ways of Washington must change," said Obama, as he laid out his platform: reshaping the economy, improving education, solving the health-care crisis, ending the Iraq War and bringing home U.S. troops stationed in the Middle East by March 2008. "I know there are those who don't believe we can do all these things," he said, before invoking Lincoln. "By ourselves, this change will not happen. Divided, we are bound to fail."

But getting past Clinton in the primaries would not be the breeze that Obama had been used to in his short but charmed political career. The New York senator enjoyed an edge in nearly all caucuses, and in the first nationally televised Democratic primary debate that April, she annihilated her opponent. When asked what the response would be to a surprise terrorist attack on the U.S., Clinton delivered a strong answer, while Obama came off "like a candidate to head the volunteer fire department," described *Time* magazine's Karen Tumulty. It got worse: By September, a poll revealed that 37 percent of Americans didn't even know who Barack Obama was.

Finally, in January 2008, nearly a year after he first announced his candidacy, the tide began to turn for Obama when he beat Clinton in the Iowa caucus. "They said this day would never come,"

"WE ARE CHOOSING HOPE OVER FEAR. WE'RE CHOOSING UNITY OVER DIVISION AND SENDING A POWERFUL MESSAGE THAT CHANGE IS COMING TO AMERICA."

—Barack Obama,
Iowa caucus victory speech

Clockwise from top left: Leaflets promoting the Obama camp were handed out at the Democratic primaries; talk-show host and friend Oprah Winfrey hit the campaign trail with Obama in December 2007; the Obama coalition attracted a wide cross-section of voter interests and backgrounds; fielding questions from reporters while en route to a rally, Obama was full of energy throughout his campaign.

Clockwise from top left: Hitting the heartland, Obama led a group of about 3,000 supporters at an Iowa rally to a steak-fry; Obama bowling during one of his long bus tours; during a 2008 Indiana visit, Obama met a cute future voter; after his early win in Iowa helped him gain recognition, he traveled the country getting to know the locals, like these Kansas City, Missouri, firefighters.

he proclaimed, describing his win as a "defining moment in history." Clinton may have been down, but she certainly wasn't out. Days later, she won New Hampshire, followed by Michigan and Nevada. The following month, on Super Tuesday—when voters in 20-plus states cast their ballots and more delegates can be won—the Clinton-Obama battle for the Democratic nomination was neck and neck: He won 13 states, while she was not far behind with eight—including the biggest, California. But just as Obama was starting to advance past his competition, controversy within his camp nearly derailed his campaign.

"CHANGE WILL NOT COME IF WE WAIT FOR SOME OTHER PERSON OR SOME OTHER TIME. WE ARE THE ONES WE'VE BEEN WAITING FOR."

—BARACK OBAMA, ON SUPER TUESDAY

In March, longtime Obama family friend Reverend Jeremiah Wright caused outrage when he gave a sermon that was perceived as both anti-America and anti-Clinton. "Hillary is married to Bill, and Bill has been good to us.... No, he ain't!" blasted Wright. "Bill did us just like he did Monica Lewinsky. He was riding dirty." Almost immediately, Obama was pressured to disassociate himself from Wright and his Trinity United Church of Christ in Chicago, but he remained loyal. "As imperfect as he may be, Reverend Wright has been like family to me," he explained at a news conference. "He strengthened my faith, officiated at my wedding and baptized my children." But when another Trinity United priest, Father Michael Pfleger, also made racially charged comments against Hillary Clinton, the presidential hopeful had no choice but to resign from Wright's congregation. "I am deeply disappointed in Father Pfleger's divisive, backward-looking rhetoric," Obama said in a statement. "This is not a decision I come to lightly. We do it with some sadness.... We don't want to have the church subjected to the scrutiny that a presidential campaign legitimately undergoes."

Although the scandal was a blemish on Obama's campaign, its effects were not lasting. In May, he beat Clinton in the North Carolina primary, effectively winning the nomination to run against Republican candidate Senator John McCain. "This fall, we intend to march forward as one Democratic Party, united by a common vision for this country," announced Obama that evening. "Because we all agree at this defining moment in history...we can't afford to give John McCain the chance to serve out George Bush's third term." Still, despite the major loss, Clinton refused to give up and carried on her campaign. It would be another month before the former first lady finally conceded to Obama via email.

With the Democratic nomination clinched, Obama's next move was selecting his running mate. Would it be Clinton? She was one of many names being tossed around, including Delaware's Senator Joe Biden, Virginia Governor Tim Kaine and Kansas Governor Kathleen Sebelius. Obama eventually narrowed it down to Clinton and Biden, with the idea that one would be his VP and the other Secretary of State. On August 23, he finally announced his decision: His running mate against McCain would be Biden, a 35-year veteran of the Senate. As for the Republican candidate, he chose relatively unknown Alaska governor Sarah Palin. Although she seemed like a random choice, Palin quickly made her presence felt to Democrats. Not only did her Republican National Convention acceptance speech pull in more TV viewers than Obama's record-breaking numbers at the Democratic National Convention, but the wife and mother attracted voters who would have cast their ballot for Clinton. Another asset for McCain was Joe the Plumber, a contractor who first garnered national attention when he confronted Obama during a campaign stop in Ohio about whether his tax plan would affect his small business. Almost overnight, Joe the Plumber became America's working-class hero—and in the third and

The presidential hopeful made calls aboard his campaign bus on December 31, 2007.

"I'M ASKING YOU TO BELIEVE, NOT JUST IN MY ABILITY TO BRING ABOUT REAL CHANGE IN WASHINGTON. I'M ASKING YOU TO BELIEVE IN YOURS."

—Barack Obama in 2008

"SENATOR OBAMA HAS ACHIEVED A GREAT THING FOR HIMSELF AND FOR HIS COUNTRY. I APPLAUD HIM FOR IT."

—JOHN McCAIN, IN HIS CONCESSION SPEECH

final presidential debate on October 15, McCain invoked his name nine times as he traded barbs with his opponent.

As Obama battled it out on the campaign trail, his family was hit by heartbreak. In October, his 86-year-old grandmother Madelyn "Toot" Dunham, who had raised him after his mother moved to Indonesia with her second husband, fell in her Honolulu apartment and broke her hip. Although she was treated and returned home, over the following two weeks, her condition deteriorated rapidly as she also battled cancer. On October 23, with the election just 12 days away, Obama hopped on a plane bound for Hawaii to spend time with Toot, who doctors predicted didn't have long to live. One of Obama's greatest regrets was not visiting his mother before she died from cancer in 1995, and he would not let history repeat itself with his grandmother. "She's gravely ill," he told ABC's *Good Morning America* after returning to the campaign trail. "We weren't sure and I'm still not sure she'll make it to Election Day. We're all praying, and we hope she does."

Sadly, Toot didn't hang on long enough. On November 3, the day before the election, Michelle called her husband with the devastating news: His beloved grandmother had passed away. But there was little time to mourn. Obama headed straight to a rally in Jacksonville, Florida, and then on to Charlotte, North Carolina, for some last-minute stumping. That evening, before a crowd of 25,000 supporters, he revealed his personal pain. "She has gone home," he said, fighting back tears. "I'm not going to talk about it too long because it's hard, a little, to talk about it."

The next morning, Obama was back in Chicago for Election Day. At 7:35 a.m., the candidate and his wife arrived at Beulah Shoesmith Elementary School to cast their votes. It was so significant to Michelle, she took her time in the voting booth to relish the moment. "I had to check out to see who she was voting for," Obama later joked. That evening, the family shared a steak dinner before they retreated to the Hyatt Regency Hotel to watch the returns with Michelle's mother and brother, the Biden family and a close-knit group of longtime friends and supporters.

Just before 10 p.m., Obama was declared the winner with 365 electoral votes to McCain's 173—yet the mood wasn't as celebratory as one would imagine. "Everybody was quiet," described Obama's mother-in-law, Marian Robinson, who held his hand during the big moment. "I can't tell you how subdued it was. We weren't like the people in the stands—you know, yelling and screaming.... It was almost like there weren't any words." Nearby, at Chicago's Grant Park, there was plenty of jubilation as more than 200,000 people cheered Obama's historic victory as America's first African American president. Their joy erupted even louder an hour later, when the first family-elect appeared onstage.

"If there is anyone out there who still doubts that America is a place where all things are possible, who still wonders if the dream of our founders is alive in our time, who still questions the power of our democracy, tonight is your answer," Obama told the crowd as he began his victory speech. He also praised his opponent and his service to the country, dating back to the Vietnam War, when the Navy officer was captured and held as a POW for five years. Calling his concession call "gracious," Obama continued, "Senator McCain fought long and hard in this campaign. And he's fought even longer and harder for the country that he loves. He has endured sacrifices for America that most of us cannot begin to imagine. We are better off for the service rendered by this brave and selfless leader."

Obama also acknowledged those closest to him who sacrificed during his campaign, especially his wife and daughters. "I would not be standing here

Clockwise from top left: During his 2008 campaign, Obama shooting hoops with the University of North Carolina team; arriving in Troy, Michigan, for a campaign town hall meeting; touring the Voith Siemens Hydro Power Plant in York, Pennsylvania, in September 2008; laughing with an Ohio supporter in October 2008 after her granddaughter mistook him for John McCain.

The iconic Obama "Hope" poster was designed by artist Shepard Fairey for the 2008 campaign.

HOPE

"I like him. I love her," Joe Biden said of the Obamas (seen here eating breakfast with him and his wife, Jill, in 2008). "She is the most impressive person I've met in 35 years."

How He Leveraged Social Media

The 2008 election was the first time candidates took their campaigns beyond the roads of America and onto the information superhighway. From the start, young Obama was an early adopter of social media, and it gave him the edge over 71-year-old McCain. Although dubbed "The Facebook Election," it was actually Twitter and MySpace that gave the Democrat the boost. In November 2008, Obama had 118,000 followers on the popular microblog (as of March 2020, he'd jumped considerably, to 113.6 million), compared to less than 5,000 for McCain. On the now-defunct MySpace, Obama had four times as many friends as his Republican opponent. His team even created a unique social platform for supporters to engage with others: my.barackobama.com. All the long hours spent surfing the web were worth it when Obama beat McCain by double the amount of electoral votes. "Were it not for the internet, Barack Obama would not be president," *Huffington Post* founder Ariana Huffington said. "I had a very optimistic feeling about [social media]," Obama agreed. "We essentially built what ended up being the most effective political campaign, probably in modern political history."

tonight without the unyielding support of my best friend for the last 16 years—the rock of our family, the love of my life, the nation's next first lady, Michelle Obama. Sasha and Malia, I love you both more than you can imagine. And you have earned the new puppy that's coming with us to the new White House. And while she's no longer with us, I know my grandmother's watching, along with the family that made me who I am. I miss them tonight. I know that my debt to them is beyond measure."

One week later, on November 10, outgoing President George W. Bush and his wife, Laura, invited the Obamas to their future home, the White House. The women bonded over their daughters as the first lady gave her successor a tour of the upstairs family quarters. Downstairs, "43" brought "44" into the Oval Office, where the two chatted about domestic and foreign affairs. A week earlier, Bush had revealed that when he called Obama to congratulate him, "I told him he can count on my complete cooperation as he makes his transition to the White House. Ensuring that this transition is seamless is a top priority for the rest of my time in office." Prior to their meeting, Obama also pledged his dedication to working with Bush. "I'm going to go in there with a spirit of bipartisanship and a sense that both the president and various leaders in Congress all recognize the severity of the situation right now and want to get stuff done."

Over the next two months, Obama worked tirelessly on his inauguration speech with chief strategist David Axelrod and speechwriter Jon Favreau. And the night before the historic January 20 event, he stayed up past midnight, reciting its lines to perfection. The next morning, the Obamas woke

Obama and Michelle voted side by side in Chicago.

"THERE WILL BE TRYING MOMENTS. THE CRITICS WILL RAGE. YOUR 'FRIENDS' WILL DISAPPOINT YOU."

—George W. Bush, in a letter to Obama

at 6 a.m. to get in a workout before the day's festivities, which began with a prayer service at St. John's Episcopal Church. It was then on to the White House, where the Bushes invited the new residents in for coffee. Michelle also brought a special gift for the outgoing first lady: a white leather journal and pen for Laura, who had signed a seven-figure book deal, to write her memoir.

At noon, Obama was sworn in as the 44th president of the U.S. at the Capitol in Washington, D.C., where 1.5 million people converged to witness history in the making. In his speech, the 47-year-old acknowledged the problems the country faced and vowed to make significant change.

"That we are in the midst of crisis is now well understood," he stated. "Our nation is at war against a far-reaching network of violence and hatred. Our economy is badly weakened, a consequence of greed and irresponsibility on the part of some but also our collective failure to make hard choices and prepare the nation for a new age. Homes have been lost, jobs shed, businesses shuttered. Our health care is too costly, our schools fail too many—and each day brings further evidence that the ways we use energy strengthen our adversaries and threaten our planet.... Today I say to you that the challenges we face are real. They are serious, and they are many. They will not be met easily or in a short span of time. But know this, America: They will be met." ○

After the election, President Bush told Obama he had "a country that is pulling for you, including me."

The Battle vs. Hillary Clinton

After eight years as first lady and seven more as a U.S. senator from New York, Hillary Clinton was intent on becoming the 44th president. In January 2007, she announced her candidacy for the Democratic nomination. "I'm in, and I'm in to win," she proclaimed. And that she did for most of the year, in early opinion polls; but when it came time to vote in the primaries in 2008, Clinton was locked in a dead heat with newcomer Obama. To turn the tide in her favor, Clinton preyed on his political inexperience, mocked his "hope and change" platform and ultimately labeled him "unelectable." Even her husband, former President Bill Clinton, jumped into the fray, accusing Obama of playing the race card and exaggerating his opposition to the Iraq War. The two opponents continued to run neck and neck until Super Tuesday, in February. Although Clinton clinched the largest states, Obama won more—yet she refused to concede. Finally, in June, Clinton ended her presidential bid and endorsed Obama at the Democratic National Convention. Despite the rivalry, Obama proved there was no bad blood when he made Clinton his administration's Secretary of State once he was elected (he even considered her to be his vice president). "We have become genuinely close," he later said, "and I could not have more respect for her."

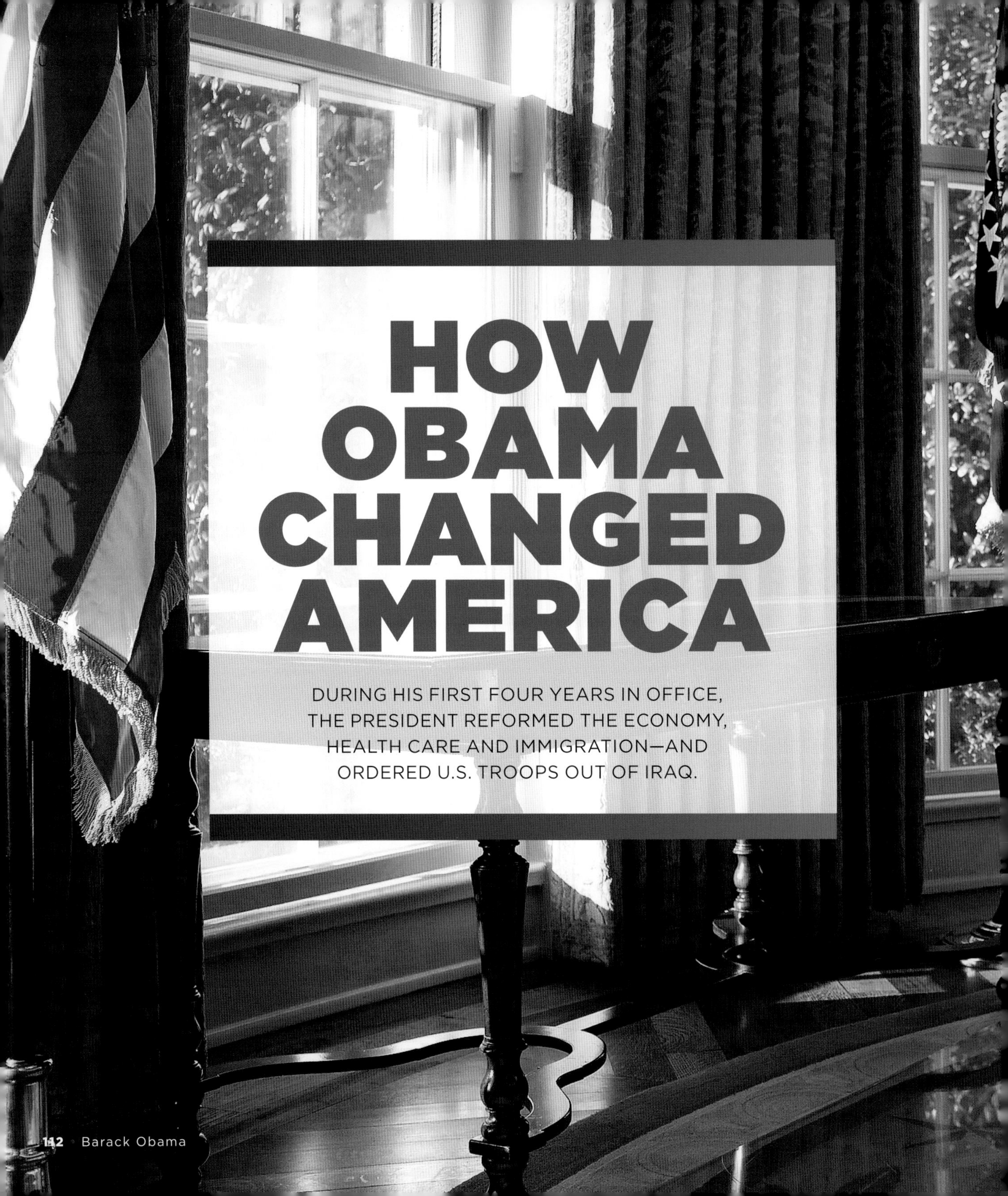

HOW OBAMA CHANGED AMERICA

DURING HIS FIRST FOUR YEARS IN OFFICE, THE PRESIDENT REFORMED THE ECONOMY, HEALTH CARE AND IMMIGRATION—AND ORDERED U.S. TROOPS OUT OF IRAQ.

“I think people forget how bad things were,” Obama (seen here on his second day in office) said about the start of his presidency.

When Barack Obama was sworn in as the 44th president of the United States on January 20, 2009, he was inheriting quite a mess. At the time, the country was engaged in two foreign wars, in Iraq and Afghanistan, and in the grips of a devastating economic recession not seen since the Great Depression of the 1930s. Unemployment was also skyrocketing: In the month he took office alone, 800,000 Americans lost their jobs. "I will say, the challenges that we're confronting are enormous, and they're multiple," Obama said at the time. "And so there are times during the course of a given day where you think, 'Where do I start?'"

He certainly didn't waste any time jumping right in. Eight days after Obama took office, his $787 billion economic-stimulus package, the American Recovery and Reinvestment Act of 2009, was passed by the House with a 244-188 vote, followed two weeks later by the Senate (61-37). The bill was designed to save existing jobs in the country and immediately create new ones—as well as provide relief to those affected by the recession. Still, unemployment continued to rise, peaking in October 2009 at 10 percent of the population. At the start of 2010, it began to decline—before growing again by the end of the year. The seesaw finally stabilized in 2012 and unemployment decreased to 7.7 percent in November, the same month Obama was reelected (in December 2013, it fell even further, to 6.7 percent). "One of the things I'm proudest about," Obama said in 2018 when looking back at his presidency, "is the fact that, within a year, we had the economy growing again, and within about a year and a half, we were actually adding jobs again instead of losing them."

During Obama's first 100 days in office, in addition to signing into law the Lilly Ledbetter Fair Pay Act and State Children's Health Insurance Program, he also issued many executive orders, some of which directly reversed policies put into place by the previous president, George W. Bush. One of those was the closing of Guantanamo Bay, a prison at the U.S. naval base in Cuba where the Bush administration housed suspected terrorists; but Congress prevented the shutdown by refusing to appropriate the required funds and blocking detainees from being relocated to the U.S. On February 27, Obama announced that U.S. combat operations in Iraq—which had cost an estimated $2 trillion and killed more than 4,400 American soldiers since Bush declared war in 2003—would end within 18 months, on August 31, 2010. "We cannot rid Iraq of all who oppose America or sympathize with our adversaries," Obama told a group of Marines preparing to deploy to Afghanistan, America's other war front following the September 11 terrorist attacks. "We cannot police Iraq's streets until they are completely safe nor stay until Iraq's union is perfected. America's men and women in uniform have fought block by block, province by province, year after year, to give the Iraqis this chance to choose a better future. Now we must ask the Iraqi people to seize it."

On the home front, Obama remained focused on rebuilding the battered economy. The American automotive industry had been ravaged by the global financial downturn that began in 2008. That year,

Obama vowed to pull troops from Iraq during a speech at North Carolina's Camp Lejeune, the largest Marine base on the East Coast.

During Obama's administration, the number of inmates held at Guantanamo Bay was reduced from approximately 245 to 41.

sales for the Big Three—General Motors, Ford Motor Company and Chrysler—fell nearly 20 percent from where they had been a decade earlier, while import auto companies grew. In December, a month after Obama was elected, then-president Bush announced a $17.4 billion bailout for the Big Three, on the basis they radically restructure in order to become profitable yet again. Once his successor took office, he created a task force to determine what to do with the trio, and in March 2009, Obama gave his mandate: If they wanted federal money, they'd have to first file for bankruptcy. GM and Chrysler agreed (Ford secured its own line of credit), so both companies could continue operating while reorganizing and thus prevent a complete collapse of the automobile industry. In exchange for the federal aid, Obama forced GM and Chrysler to adopt stricter fuel-economy standards. The government also managed the sale of Chrysler to Italian automaker Fiat.

The decision to bail out GM and Chrysler was unpopular with many Americans, who felt the corporations responsible for the recession—which resulted in millions of citizens losing their jobs and homes—were being rescued instead of punished. In a CNN poll, only 37 percent supported the bailout. But Obama believed it was a necessary evil to prevent even more unemployment, since more than 1.5 million jobs depended on the Big Three. And he was right: In 2011, sales rose 10 percent for GM, 13 percent for Ford and 14 percent for Chrysler (then known as Fiat Chrysler Automobiles), in addition to boosting employment for carmakers and parts suppliers by 250,000. "If GM and Chrysler would've gone into free fall," explained

"EXPERTS FROM ACROSS THE POLITICAL SPECTRUM WARNED IF WE DIDN'T ACT, WE MIGHT FACE A SECOND DEPRESSION. SO WE ACTED... AND ONE YEAR LATER, THE WORST OF THE STORM HAS PASSED."

—Barack Obama, in 2010

Scores of 2009 Ford F-150 trucks sat unsold in a Detroit lot until the auto bailout.

Ford CEO Alan Mulally in 2012, "they could've taken the entire supply base into free fall also—and taken the U.S. from a recession into a depression." During a 2015 speech at a Ford plant just outside of Detroit, Obama praised his polarizing decision. "It was not popular—even in Michigan," he revealed to a group of workers. "Betting on you was the right thing to do. That bet has paid off for America, because the American auto industry is back."

Despite Americans' unhappiness with the auto industry bailout, at the end of Obama's first 100 days in April 2009, his approval rating was 63 percent, the fourth-highest since John F. Kennedy in 1961 and the highest since Jimmy Carter in 1977. (By comparison, Ronald Reagan scored 60 percent in 1981; George H. W. Bush, 57 percent in 1989; Bill Clinton, 55 percent in 1993; George W. Bush, 58 percent in 2001; and Donald J. Trump, 42 percent in 2017). "The first hundred days is going to be important," noted Obama, "but it's probably going to be the first thousand days that makes the difference."

Indeed, his next 900 days, which covered most of his first term, were equally impressive—beginning with a historic change to the Supreme Court. In May 2009, he appointed Sonia Sotomayor to replace retiring Associate Justice David Souter, making her the court's first judge of Hispanic descent (she was confirmed in a 68-31 Senate vote). Describing Sotomayor as "an inspiring woman who I believe will make a great justice," Obama explained she "has worked at almost every level of our judicial system, providing her with a depth of experience and a breadth of perspective that will be invaluable as a Supreme Court justice." A year later, he nominated Elena Kagan, who was confirmed 63-37, bringing the total number of women sitting simultaneously on the Court to three, for the first time.

In 2010, Elena Kagan became the fourth woman appointed to the Supreme Court.

"I DO NOT ACCEPT SECOND PLACE FOR THE UNITED STATES OF AMERICA... IT'S TIME TO GET SERIOUS ABOUT FIXING THE PROBLEMS THAT ARE HAMPERING OUR GROWTH."

—BARACK OBAMA

Throughout the remainder of President Obama's first term, he brought reform to a number of issues, including the environment, health care and LGBT rights. In October 2009, he signed the Matthew Shepard and James Byrd Jr. Hate Crimes Prevention Act, which expanded a 1969 federal law to include crimes motivated by a victim's sexual orientation or gender identity. That same month, he also lifted the ban on travel to the U.S. by people infected with HIV. In March 2010, Obama signed perhaps his most important federal statute, the Patient Protection

A year before Kagan, the third female justice, Sonia Sotomayor, was appointed after receiving strong public support from first lady Michelle Obama.

The president signed the Affordable Care Act on March 23, 2010, in the White House's East Room.

THE LEGACY OF OBAMACARE

While campaigning for the 2008 election, Obama had promised "to make health care affordable and available for every single American." And once he was elected, he wasted no time working to make it a reality for the estimated 45 million citizens who did not have insurance. During the summer and fall of 2009, the president's Patient Protection and Affordable Care Act, often shortened to the Affordable Care Act, was hotly debated in Congress and lobbied against by insurance companies, worried their business would be affected by the reform. Finally, after making some amendments on his proposed bill, both houses of Congress passed it, and on March 23, 2010, Obama signed it into law. He told the press gathered in the White House's East Room that the moment was "on behalf of my mother, who argued with insurance companies even as she battled cancer in her final days."

The Affordable Care Act, now known as Obamacare, made history as the most significant expansion of the U.S. health-care system since the passage of Medicare and Medicaid in 1965. Under it, those with preexisting conditions could not be rejected by insurance companies; contraceptive care was free; and families were able to keep children up to the age of 26 on their insurance. Obamacare reduced the number of uninsured Americans by 20 million; and, according to a study conducted at Harvard University, it saves tens of thousands of lives every year.

But once Obama's presidency ended in January 2017 and Donald J. Trump took office, House Republicans immediately began to devise a plan to repeal Obamacare, and on March 6 announced their replacement, The American Health Care Act. Although the House of Representatives voted to pass it (albeit by a narrow margin of 217-213), it was struck down in the Senate when three Republicans, including John McCain, who was battling brain cancer at the time, sided with Democrats. Although he was lobbied strongly by Vice President Mike Pence to repeal Obamacare, McCain famously gave a dramatic thumbs-down when asked to cast his vote.

But ten years after its 2010 passage, Obamacare is still on the firing line. The Supreme Court will ultimately decide whether a lower court ruling that made the mandates unconstitutional should hold.

"IT TOOK A LOT OF BLOOD, SWEAT AND TEARS TO GET WHERE WE ARE TODAY, BUT WE HAVE JUST BEGUN."

—Barack Obama

After the NYPD clashed with Occupy Wall Street protestors, another group rallied against the brutality in Manhattan's One Police Plaza on September 30, 2011.

and Affordable Care Act, an amendment to a 1944 public health act known as Obamacare that radically reformed the U.S. health-care system (learn more about Obamacare on page 121) and guaranteed coverage to all Americans. The following month, the president announced his space policy at Kennedy Space Center in Cape Canaveral, Florida, and committed to increasing NASA funding by $6 billion. He also promised $40 million to help Space Coast workers affected by the retirement of the Space Shuttle program after nearly four decades. In December, Obama banned new drilling in the eastern Gulf of Mexico for at least seven years, a result of the April 2010 explosion of BP's Deepwater Horizon rig, which killed 11 people and dumped an estimated 206 million gallons of oil into the region over the course of three months, making it one of the worst environmental disasters in U.S. history. Obama closed out 2010 by repealing 1993's Don't Ask, Don't Tell policy that had prevented gay and lesbian Americans from serving openly in the military.

Although President Obama had made great strides in restoring the economy and lowering unemployment, by 2011 there was still so much that needed to be done to financially revive the country. On September 8, in a nationally televised speech before Congress that was broadcast on 11 networks, he proposed the American Jobs Act, a $447 billion stimulus plan that would include breaks for small business and cuts in payroll taxes as well as provide funds to repair roads and bridges, which would then create construction jobs. Obama spent weeks touring the country to promote the bill, but in the end, Republicans, as well as some Democrats, voted it down, citing its plan to take away tax breaks for wealthy citizens. At the time, many Americans, primarily the middle class, were still smarting from the bailouts that had benefited big business, the same people Congress was once again protecting—and unrest began to brew.

On September 17, a protest movement called Occupy Wall Street (OWS) took over Zuccotti Park in New York City's financial district to bring awareness to economic inequality. Their slogan, "We are the 99%," referenced the 1 percent of Americans who earned more than one-fifth of the entire population's income, many of whom were the bankers, hedge-fund managers and business leaders responsible for the bad decisions that brought on the recession in 2007. The remaining 99 percent, OWS protestors argued, were the ones who truly suffered during that time. Now, they were demanding a more-balanced distribution of income, more and better jobs, bank reform, forgiveness of student loan debt and aid for the rash of home foreclosures across the country. On October 6, weeks into the protest, President Obama addressed OWS. "I think it expresses the frustrations the American people feel, that we had the biggest financial crisis since the Great Depression, huge collateral damage all throughout the country...and yet you're still seeing some of the same folks who acted irresponsibly trying to fight efforts to crack down on the abusive practices that got us into this in the first place."

As Obama campaigned for his reelection in 2012, he took on an issue that had long divided the nation: immigration reform. On June 15, the president announced he was taking executive action and that his administration would no longer deport undocumented immigrants who matched criteria found in the DREAM (Development, Relief, and Education for Alien Minors) Act, which was first proposed in 2001 but had failed to pass. Under Obama's new policy, Deferred Action for Childhood Arrivals (DACA), illegal immigrants under the age of 31 who had been brought into the U.S. as children before their 16th birthday could apply to be eligible for a higher education and permanent residency. Furthermore, children born in the U.S. would automatically become American citizens by "birthright," even if their parents entered the country illegally. "I take executive action only when we have a serious problem, a serious issue, and Congress chooses to do nothing," Obama explained. "And in this situation, the failure of House Republicans to pass a darn bill is bad for our security, it's bad for our economy and it's bad for our future." On August 15, the U.S. Citizenship and Immigration Services began accepting applications for the DACA program, with approximately 88 percent of them being approved. By the end of Obama's presidency in January 2017, 740,000 people had registered under DACA—a policy his successor Donald Trump rescinded eight months later.

Although Obama had countless successes during his first four years in office, he made it clear while campaigning for his reelection in 2012 that four more years was necessary to truly bring about the hope and change he had promised Americans during the 2008 election. "We've got a lot more work to do," the president told supporters at a rally in Davenport, Iowa. "We've got unfinished business to attend to. I've come here to ask you to stand with me and help me finish the job. I'm asking you to help finish what we started, to bring about the change that is going to make America live up to its promise, not just for this generation, but for generations to come. That is why I am running for a second term as president of the United States of America.... I told you four years ago, I said, don't look for quick fixes. We didn't get into this overnight; we're not going to solve it overnight. But what I said, and what is still true, is we've got all the things we need, all the ingredients. We've got the capacity to meet our challenges."

Death of Osama bin Laden

Ever since the September 11, 2001, terrorist attacks that killed 2,977 Americans, the U.S. government had been on a manhunt for its mastermind, Osama bin Laden. After a nearly 10-year search, the CIA learned the al-Qaeda leader was hiding in Pakistan, near the capital city of Islamabad—and on May 1, 2011, Obama ordered the U.S. Navy SEALs to raid bin Laden's compound. Hours later, the president and his national security team, including Vice President Joe Biden and Secretary of State Hillary Clinton, gathered in the White House's Situation Room to watch the event unfold in real time via night-vision images taken by a drone.

Less than 40 minutes later, bin Laden was discovered hiding in a third-floor bedroom, using his youngest wife, Amal, as a human shield. Within seconds, SEAL Team Six member Robert O'Neill shot the terrorist three times in the head, killing him instantly. Observing back in Washington, D.C., Obama exclaimed, "We got him!" After confirming the body was indeed that of bin Laden, in accordance with Islamic tradition he was buried at sea within 24 hours of his death and photos of his corpse were never released.

On May 8, President Obama opened up about the secret mission in a candid interview with *60 Minutes*. Although he revealed he was "nervous" about the operation, he insisted that "the one thing I didn't lose sleep over was the possibility of taking bin Laden out. Justice was done. And I think that anyone who would question that the perpetrator of mass murder on American soil didn't deserve what he got needs to have their head examined."

"CHANGE IS HARD, CHANGE TAKES TIME, BUT CHANGE IS POSSIBLE."

—Barack Obama, to supporters at a reelection rally in October 2011

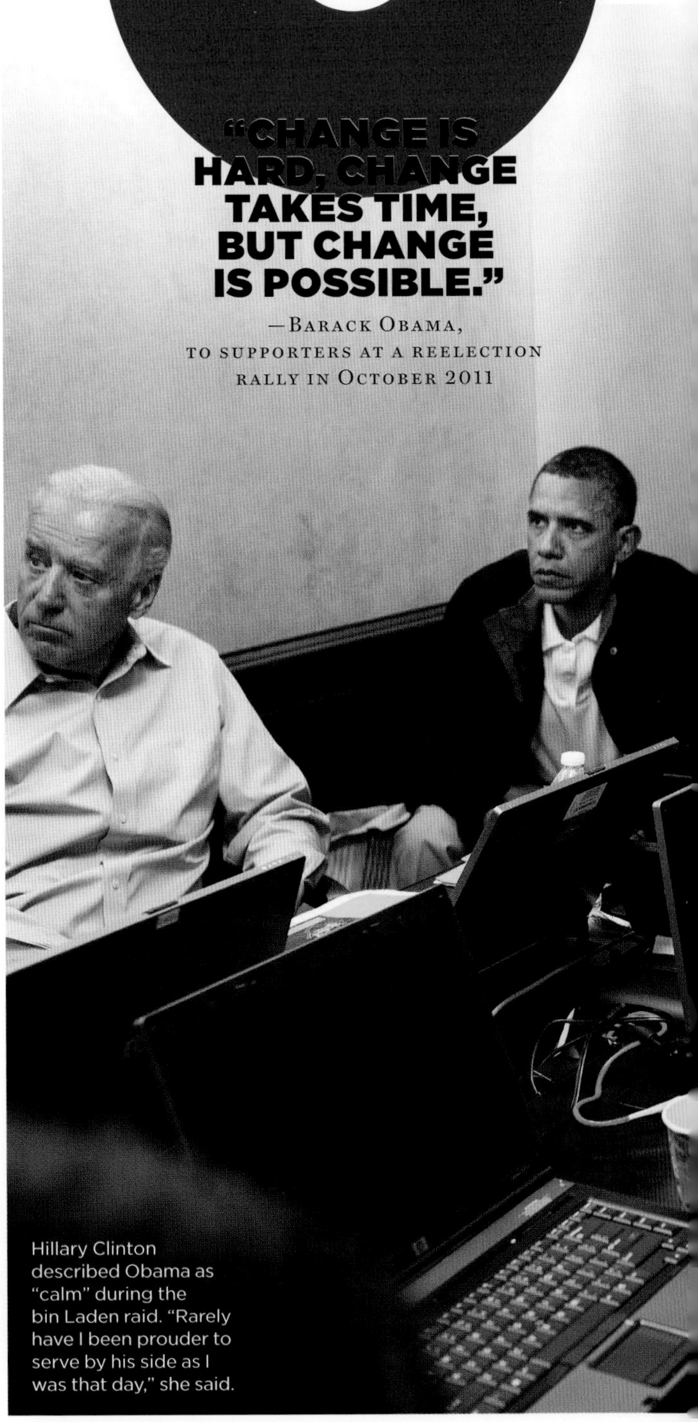

Hillary Clinton described Obama as "calm" during the bin Laden raid. "Rarely have I been prouder to serve by his side as I was that day," she said.

Four More Years

IN THE 2012 ELECTION, OBAMA EASILY DEFEATED MITT ROMNEY, BUT FACED CHALLENGES WITH FOREIGN POLICIES.

When President Obama was re-elected on November 6, 2012, he thanked "America's happy warrior," Vice President Biden.

"HE HAS DONE A GOOD JOB WITH A BAD HAND."

—Former President Bill Clinton, on Obama

When President Barack Obama announced his plans to seek a second term in April 2011, 20 months before the 2012 election, he did so in the most 21st-century way. Instead of a traditional speech—like he'd given on the steps of the Old State Capitol Building in Springfield, Illinois, in February 2007, surrounded by wife Michelle and daughters Malia and Sasha—Obama dropped his news via an internet campaign that included an email, social media posts and a YouTube video.

"Today, we are filing papers to launch our 2012 campaign," he said in an official statement. "We're doing this now because the politics we believe in do not start with expensive TV ads or extravaganzas but with you—with people organizing block by block, talking to neighbors, co-workers and friends. And that kind of campaign takes time to build. So even though I'm focused on the job you elected me to do, and the race may not reach full speed for a year or more, the work of laying the foundation for our campaign must start today."

Getting the Democratic nomination was a surefire bet, with no other candidates on the ballot in all but seven states in the primaries. That allowed Obama to focus on running the country as Republicans, including Senator John McCain, former Massachusetts Governor Mitt Romney, former Speaker of the House Newt Gingrich and former Pennsylvania senator Rick Santorum, battled it out for the chance to oppose him. In August 2012, delegates at the Republican National Convention officially nominated Romney, who named U.S. Representative from Wisconsin Paul Ryan as his running mate. Weeks later, the Obama-Biden ticket was formally announced at the Democratic National Convention by former President Bill Clinton.

For an unprecedented 48 minutes, the husband of then Secretary of State Hillary Clinton outlined all of Obama's wins during his first term, including bringing the country back from the brink of an economic depression, securing health care for all Americans and reforming immigration laws. "My fellow Americans, you have to decide what kind of country you want to live in," said Clinton. "If you want a you're-on-your-own, winner-take-all society, you should support the Republican ticket. If you want a country of shared opportunities and shared responsibilities—a 'we're all in it together' society, you should vote for Barack Obama and Joe Biden.... I love our country—and I know we're coming back. For more than 200 years, through every crisis, we've always come out stronger than we went in. And we will again, as long as we do it together. We champion the cause for which our founders pledged their lives, their fortunes, their sacred honor—to form a more perfect union. If that's what you believe, if that's what you want, we have to reelect President Barack Obama."

But just eight days before the election, the entire eastern seaboard of the U.S., from Maine to Florida, was pummeled by Hurricane Sandy, killing nearly 100 people and causing $65 billion in damage. Both Obama and Romney put their campaigns on hold and the president flew to New Jersey, one of the hardest-hit areas, to offer his support. Photos of Obama surveying the damage with Republican Governor Chris Christie, one of his most vocal opponents, was a bipartisan dream scenario that only bolstered his already-strong chances of being reelected.

Sure enough, on November 6, Obama defeated Romney 332 electoral votes to 206, with 51.1 percent of the popular vote. "Tonight, despite all the hardship we've been through, despite all the frustrations of Washington, I've never been more hopeful about our future," Obama proclaimed to the nation after his win.

Obama was the first president to support same-sex marriage.

Why He Changed His Mind on Same-Sex Marriage

President Obama pushed for the Supreme Court to legalize same-sex marriage in 2015, but he didn't always support it. In 1998, while seeking reelection to the Illinois Senate, he said he was "undecided" on the issue. Six years later, while campaigning for the U.S. Senate, it seemed he had made up his mind. "Marriage is between a man and a woman," he said in a TV interview. "We have a set of traditions in place that I think needs to be preserved." In his 2006 book *The Audacity of Hope*, Obama recalled how that stance, which he credited to his faith, had hurt the feelings of one of his biggest supporters, a lesbian. "I felt bad," he wrote. "I was reminded that it is my obligation, not only as an elected official in a pluralistic society but also as a Christian, to remain open to the possibility that my unwillingness to support gay marriage is misguided." Still, in 2008, while running for president, he said, "I believe that marriage is the union between a man and a woman."

But once in office, his opinion changed. In 2010, he acknowledged: "Attitudes evolve, including mine. And it is an issue that I wrestle with and think about because I have a whole host of friends who are in gay partnerships. I have staff members who are in committed, monogamous relationships, who are raising children, who are wonderful parents. And I care about them deeply."

In May 2012, as more states banned same-sex marriage, POTUS declared his position decisively in an ABC News interview. "It is important for me to affirm I think same-sex couples should be able to get married," he told Robin Roberts. Obama credited his new stance to his daughters, who believed their friends with same-sex parents shouldn't be treated differently: "It doesn't make sense to them, and...that's the kind of thing that prompts a change in perspective."

Finally, on June 26, 2015, the Supreme Court ruled same-sex marriage was legal in all 50 states, a move Obama called a "victory for America." That evening, in celebration of the decision, the White House was lit with rainbow-colored lights.

"And I ask you to sustain that hope. I'm not talking about blind optimism, the kind of hope that just ignores the enormity of the tasks ahead or the roadblocks that stand in our path. I'm not talking about the wishful idealism that allows us to just sit on the sidelines or shirk from a fight. I have always believed that hope is that stubborn thing inside us that insists, despite all the evidence to the contrary, that something better awaits us, so long as we have the courage to keep reaching, to keep working, to keep fighting."

Obama's words were put to the test just weeks later on December 14, 2012, the day he has described as the worst of his entire presidency. That morning, 20 first-grade children and six adults were killed in a mass shooting at Sandy Hook Elementary School in Newtown, Connecticut. The president grieved the tragedy, and Pete Souza, the official White House photographer, recalled it was the first time he had ever seen him cry. In a press briefing, Obama wiped tears from his eyes as he addressed the nation. "They had their entire lives ahead of them—birthdays, graduations, weddings, kids of their own," he said somberly. "In the hard days to come, that community needs us to be at our best as Americans. And I will do everything in my power as president to help."

The president embraced Jackie Barden, whose son Daniel was killed in the Sandy Hook massacre.

Obama honored his promise on January 5, 2013, when he announced 23 gun-control executive orders, including background checks on all gun sales. He urged Congress not to overturn his proposal and they didn't. (President Donald J. Trump revoked the order in February 2017, much to the praise of the National Rifle Association.) "Once Congress gets on board with commonsense gun safety measures, we can reduce gun violence a whole lot more," he said. "But we also can't wait. Until we have a Congress that's in line with the majority of Americans, there are actions within my legal authority that we can take to help reduce gun violence and save more lives—actions that protect our rights and our kids.... And, yes, it will be hard, and it won't happen overnight. It won't happen during this Congress. It won't happen during my presidency. But a lot of things don't happen overnight. So just because it's hard, that's no excuse not to try."

"THE GUN LOBBY MAY BE HOLDING CONGRESS HOSTAGE RIGHT NOW, BUT THEY CANNOT HOLD AMERICA HOSTAGE."

—BARACK OBAMA, ON GUN CONTROL

Although Obama had benefited from a Democrat-controlled Senate during his first term and the first half of his second, Republicans took over both houses of Congress in November 2014. The president shifted his focus from domestic issues, like unemployment, health care and immigration, to foreign affairs, specifically in the Middle East. Although Obama had ordered all troops out of Iraq, after extremist Islamic group ISIS launched an attack on Northern Iraq and captured many of its key cities in June 2014, the U.S. was one of the U.N. member states to get involved. The president pledged to deploy 275 soldiers to provide security at

"I saw my normally stoic boss break down," press secretary Jay Carney said of Obama after the Sandy Hook shooting.

Clockwise from top left: Russia was increasingly worrisome to Obama (here, with President Vladimir Putin in 2015); U.S. troops helped Iraq fight ISIS in October 2016; "I don't like him; I love him," Joe Biden said when Obama awarded him the Medal of Freedom in January 2017; two days after the 2016 election, Obama met with Donald Trump at the White House.

> **"EIGHT YEARS LATER, I AM EVEN MORE OPTIMISTIC ABOUT OUR COUNTRY'S PROMISE."**
>
> —Barack Obama, in 2016

the U.S. Embassy in Baghdad but insisted he would not send American troops "back into combat in Iraq." That August, as ISIS grew more violent—the group had captured and beheaded American journalist James Wright Foley—Obama decided to defend Iraq with air strikes against the extremists, a move that was backed by both Republicans and Democrats in Congress, even though there was fear ISIS might seek revenge.

Syria was another country in need of U.S. help, after civil war broke out in 2011 between President Bashar al-Assad and anti-government rebels. In August 2012, Obama threatened al-Assad with retaliation if chemical weapons were used against the Syrian people. "We have been very clear to the Assad regime," he said, "that a red line for us is, we start seeing a whole bunch of chemical weapons moving around or being utilized. That would change my calculus." A year to the day later, it was reported that al-Assad had killed more than a thousand people in Damascus with sarin gas—yet the U.S. did nothing. As a result, Obama's failure to enforce his "red line" became a black mark on his presidency.

Russia was another country proving to be a menace for America. Obama, much like George W. Bush before him, wasn't on the best of terms with President Vladimir Putin (Obama once said the Russian leader looked like "the bored kid in the back of the classroom" during one of their meetings). But any hopes for a relationship vanished in August 2013, when Putin provided asylum to Edward Snowden, the former U.S. government contractor who leaked classified spy information about the National Security Agency.

During an appearance on *The Tonight Show with Jay Leno*, Obama said he was "disappointed" in Putin's betrayal. "It's reflective of some underlying challenges we've had with Russia lately," he added. "A lot of what's been going on hasn't been major breaks in the relationship.... But there have been times where they slip back into Cold War thinking and a Cold War mentality. And what I consistently say to them and...to President Putin, is that's the past and we've got to think about the future. There's no reason why we shouldn't be able to cooperate more effectively than we do."

While not all Americans can agree on Obama's historic presidency and his policies, he arguably left things better than he'd found them in January 2009. At the time, the U.S. was faced with the possibility of a severe economic setback and embroiled in two long, expensive and deadly wars. When Obama left office in January 2017, the nation's unemployment rate had declined from 7.8 percent to 4.7 percent; the number of Americans without health insurance was cut in half; the Dow Jones average more than doubled; fewer people were living below the poverty line; and the number of troops stationed in Iraq and Afghanistan was reduced by a staggering 91 percent.

"That's why I leave this stage tonight even more optimistic about this country than I was when we started," President Obama expressed during his farewell speech on January 10, 2017, in Chicago. "Because I know our work has not only helped so many Americans; it has inspired so many Americans—especially so many young people out there—to believe you can make a difference; to hitch your wagon to something bigger than yourselves. This generation coming up—unselfish, altruistic, creative, patriotic—I've seen you in every corner of the country. You believe in a fair, just, inclusive America; you know that constant change has been America's hallmark, something not to fear but to embrace, and you are willing to carry this hard work of democracy forward. You'll soon outnumber any of us, and I believe, as a result, the future is in good hands."

In his final remarks as president, Obama concluded with a promise: "My fellow Americans, it has been the honor of my life to serve you. I won't stop; in fact, I will be right there with you, as a citizen, for all my days that remain."

A Special Friendship With Joe Biden

Over their eight years leading America, President Obama and Vice President Joe Biden enjoyed a friendship far beyond politics. Once Obama chose the veteran senator as his running mate, the two men and their families quickly bonded. Not only did first lady Michelle Obama and second lady Jill Biden grow close, but so did the Obama daughters and Biden granddaughters. The Obamas were also there during the hard times. When Biden's son Beau, the Attorney General of Delaware, suffered a stroke in 2010 and faced the prospect of having to step down, thus losing his annual salary, the Bidens considered selling their home to support Beau's family—but the president wouldn't hear of it. "He said, 'Promise me you won't sell the house,'" Biden revealed. "'I'll give you the money.'" Although Beau recovered, he died five years later from brain cancer. At his funeral, Obama gave the eulogy: "We are here to grieve with you," he said, "but more importantly, we are here because we love you." Days before the end of his presidency, Obama surprised his "brother" with the nation's highest civilian honor, the Presidential Medal of Freedom with Distinction. When Biden realized what was happening, he turned his back to the audience and wiped away tears. "Mr. President, you know as long as there's a breath in me, I'll be there for you," he promised that day. "And I know, I know it is reciprocal." Although Obama dissuaded Biden from running for president in 2016, Biden announced his candidacy for 2020—but the Obamas didn't immediately voice their support. "Barack and I are not endorsing in the primary," explained Michelle, "because we want to support whoever wins."

"He makes up for a lot more of my shortcomings than I do his," Biden has said of Obama.

BECOMING FIRST LADY

IN HER FIRST MEMOIR, MICHELLE OBAMA PULLED BACK THE CURTAIN ON HER LIFE—BEFORE, DURING AND AFTER THE WHITE HOUSE—AND GOT CANDID ABOUT THE CHALLENGES SHE FACED.

"I WAS HUMBLED AND EXCITED TO BE FIRST LADY, BUT NOT FOR ONE SECOND DID I THINK I'D BE SLIDING INTO SOME GLAMOROUS, EASY ROLE."
—Michelle Obama

During a signing in New York City, a supporter was overcome with emotion upon meeting the former first lady.

The Obamas share a "special fondness" for Queen Elizabeth II: "She showed me that humanity is more important than protocol or formality."

Military families were important to Michelle, and she honored them with a special concert in January 2013.

FOR EIGHT YEARS, MICHELLE OBAMA SERVED AS THE FIRST LADY BESIDE HER HUSBAND, PRESIDENT BARACK OBAMA, AND WAS A CONSTANT SOURCE OF CLASS, DIGNITY, STRENGTH AND INSPIRATION.

But behind her public exterior, not everything was picture-perfect. In her best-selling memoir, *Becoming*, she offered readers a look at the highs and lows: everything from marriage and motherhood to the campaign trail and life in the White House.

Becoming, which sold a record-breaking 1.4 million copies in the first week of its November 2018 release, is divided into three sections: Becoming Me (childhood and early career); Becoming Us (Barack and their daughters, Malia and Sasha); and Becoming More (as the first family). "There is no handbook for incoming first ladies of the United States," she explains. "It's not technically a job, nor is it an official government title. It comes with no salary and no spelled-out set of obligations. It's a strange kind of sidecar to the presidency, a seat that by the time I came to it had already been occupied by more than forty-three different women, each of whom had done it in her own way."

Before they even made it to the White House, Michelle was feeling the intense scrutiny of the spotlight out on the campaign trail. Cast in the media as an "angry black woman," she drew more fire in February 2008 when she told a crowd of supporters at a Milwaukee rally, "For the first time in my adult lifetime, I'm really proud of my country." To many, the perception was the potential first lady of the United States wasn't proud to be an American, a claim her husband adamantly dismissed. "What she meant," Obama explained at the time, "was this is the first time she's been proud of the politics of America." In *Becoming*, Michelle clarifies the damning clip that circulated all over the news was only 10 seconds of a 40-minute speech, and taken out of context. "Here was the first punch. And I'd seemingly brought it on myself. In trying to speak casually, I'd forgotten how weighted each little phrase could be. Unwittingly, I'd given the haters a fourteen-word feast.... I flew home to Chicago that night, feeling guilty and dispirited."

The backlash was especially hurtful considering Michelle wasn't thrilled about her husband's decision to run for president in the first place. Two years earlier, when she spotted him on the cover of *Time* magazine with the headline "Why Barack Obama could be the next president," she reveals, "[I] had to turn my head away." She continues, "What I hoped was that at some point Barack himself would put an end to the speculation, declaring himself out of contention and directing the media gaze elsewhere. But he didn't do this. He wouldn't do this. He wanted to run. He wanted it and I didn't. Anytime a reporter asked whether he'd join the race for president, Barack would demur, saying simply, 'I'm still thinking about it. It's a family decision.' Which was code for 'Only if Michelle says I can.'"

Bo and Sunny were free to roam throughout much of the White House. Their favorite spots were the garden and kitchen.

In June 2015, the first lady led a Let Girls Learn event in London, which aimed to expand education for girls around the world.

Much to her chagrin, she remained in the crosshairs even after becoming the first lady, oftentimes for the most innocuous of infractions. Just three months on the job in April 2009, the Obamas traveled abroad to attend the G20 summit in England, where they first met with Queen Elizabeth II. Although it was a momentous occasion for Michelle "coming face-to-face with an honest-to-goodness icon," critics slammed her fashion accessory, a cardigan draped over her knee-length black dress. "You don't go to Buckingham Palace in a sweater," schooled designer Oscar de la Renta in a *Women's Wear Daily* interview.

Later that evening, the first lady made a second faux pas during a one-on-one moment with the Queen. As the two were bonding over their uncomfortable high heels, "I then did what's instinctive to me anytime I feel connected to a new person, which is to express my feelings outwardly," explains Michelle. "I laid a hand affectionately across her shoulder… I'd touched the Queen of England, which I'd soon learn was apparently not done. Our interaction at the reception was caught on camera, and in the coming days it would be reproduced in media reports all over the world: 'A Breach in Protocol!' 'Michelle Obama Dares to Hug the Queen!'" As Kate Betts wrote in her book *Everyday Icon*, "Half of England nearly had a stroke." Michelle continues, "It revived some of the campaign-era speculation that I was generally uncouth and lacking the standard elegance of a first lady, and worried me somewhat, too, thinking I'd possibly distracted from Barack's efforts abroad. But I tried not to let the criticism rattle me. If I hadn't done the proper thing at Buckingham Palace, I had at least done the human thing. I daresay that the Queen was okay with it, too, because when I touched her, she only pulled closer, resting a gloved hand lightly on the small of my back."

Even the first lady's passion project, Let's Move!, an anti-childhood-obesity campaign that encouraged healthier food in schools and more physical activity, somehow drew criticism, although mostly from conservatives. (Talk-show host Rush Limbaugh rebuked, "It doesn't look like [she] follows her own nutritionary, dietary advice. And then we hear that she's out eating ribs at 1,500 calories a serving with 141 grams of fat per serving.") Despite its detractors, the program was a success: Within a year, 6,000 salad bars had been installed in school cafeterias; mayors from 500 cities and towns committed to tackle childhood obesity; and

Michelle's Accomplishments

THE FIRST LADY HAS SO MUCH TO BE PROUD OF IN HER LIFE.

IVY LEAGUE EDUCATION

Although neither of her parents graduated from college, Michelle LaVaughn Robinson earned degrees from not one but two Ivy League universities: a BA at Princeton, followed by a JD from Harvard Law School.

SUCCESSFUL CAREER

The attorney worked as a law associate until she got married, when she segued into city government jobs and then to high-profile positions at both the University of Chicago and the University of Chicago Hospitals.

SUPPORTIVE WIFE

Throughout her husband's career, first as an Illinois State Senator and then as president, Michelle was by his side, campaigning, giving speeches and working to ensure victory—even though it often kept him away from their family.

DEVOTED MOTHER

Juggling family and career with her husband's political aspirations was difficult at times, but being a mother made it all worth it. "Malia and Sasha's bond has always been tight," Michelle writes. "And their cuteness still melts my heart."

TIRELESS ADVOCATE

As first lady, she brought awareness to health, women's rights and education. In 2018, her nonpartisan organization, When We All Vote, traveled the country, urging all to register to vote ahead of the midterm elections.

"I TRIED AS OFTEN AS POSSIBLE TO BE HOME TO GREET THE GIRLS WHEN THEY CAME BACK FROM SCHOOL. IT WAS ONE BENEFIT OF LIVING ABOVE THE OFFICE."

—MICHELLE OBAMA, ON BALANCING FIRST LADY DUTIES AND MOTHERHOOD

"IF YOU DON'T GET OUT THERE AND DEFINE YOURSELF, YOU'LL BE QUICKLY AND INACCURATELY DEFINED BY OTHERS."

—Michelle Obama

Michelle stopped by *Jimmy Kimmel Live!* to promote her memoir.

Sesame Street characters helped promote the Let's Move! campaign.

In December 2019, Michelle traveled to Vietnam to promote girls' education with the Obama Foundation's Girls Opportunity Alliance.

Walmart pledged to cut the amount of sugar, salt and fat in its food products (and reduce the price on its stores' produce). Additionally, in 2010, Michelle worked to push a new child-nutrition bill through Congress. Let's Move! became a real sense of pride for the first lady. "I was beginning to realize that all the things that felt odd to me about my new existence—the strangeness of fame, the hawkeyed attention paid to my image, the vagueness of my job description—could be marshaled in service of real goals. I was energized. Here, finally, was a way to show my full self."

Throughout *Becoming*, there are many passages about the Obamas' relationship, from her first impression of Barack ("a guy with a big smile and a whiff of geekiness") to the stresses of caring for their daughters without her husband as he focused on his political career. "At home, our frustrations began to rear up often and intensely," writes Michelle. "Barack and I loved each other deeply, but it was as if at the center of our relationship there were suddenly a knot we couldn't loosen." At the time, during Obama's tenure in the Illinois Senate, "I was thirty-eight years old and had seen other marriages come undone in a way that made me feel protective of ours." In the hopes of not becoming another statistic, Michelle suggested couples counseling, something her husband was "reluctant" to try. "Sitting down in front of a stranger struck him as uncomfortable, if not a tad dramatic. Couldn't he just run over to Borders and buy some relationship books?" But once they did begin to meet with a therapist, "Slowly, over hours of talking, the knot began to loosen. Each time Barack and I left his office, we felt a bit more connected." After leaving the White House, "We are finding each other again," she told *People* in 2018. "We have dinners alone and chunks of time where it's just us—what we were when we started this thing: no kids, no publicity, no nothing. Just us and our dreams."

In her book—which has sold more than 11.7 million copies and won a Grammy for Best Spoken Word Album in 2020 for its audio book—there are also plenty of private glimpses of the first parents. When eldest daughter Malia was invited to the prom, the 16-year-old begged the president and first lady to "be cool" when her date, a boy she had a crush on, arrived at the White House to pick her up. "I was barefoot, and Barack was in flip-flops," Michelle recalled. "Barack and I shook the young man's hand, snapped a few pictures, and gave our daughter a hug before sending them on their way. We took what was perhaps unfair comfort in the knowledge that Malia's security detail would basically ride the boy's bumper all the way to the restaurant where they were going for dinner before the dance and would remain on quiet duty throughout the night." Michelle also recalls attending Parents' Night at Sidwell Friends School when Sasha was in third grade and coming across her younger daughter's "What I Did on My Summer Vacation" essay hanging on a wall. "I went to Rome and I met the Pope," Sasha had written. "He was missing part of his thumb." Her mother couldn't help but be amused. "We'd taken an observant, matter-of-fact eight-year-old to Rome, Moscow, and Accra, and this is what she'd brought back."

"IT IS TRUE, MY WIFE IS SMARTER, BETTER-LOOKING.... IF I'M A 10, MICHELLE'S AN 11."

—Barack Obama

Protecting Malia and Sasha's privacy was crucial to the Obamas, and in order to do that, they had to get creative "finding other ways to satiate the public's curiosity about our family," explains Michelle. "Early in Barack's second term, we'd added a new puppy to the household—Sunny—a free-spirited rambler who seemed to see no point in being house-trained, given how big her new house was.... The dogs added a lightness to everything." Sunny and Bo happily took over their big sisters' roles. "Knowing that Malia and Sasha were basically off-limits, the White House communications teams began requesting the dogs for official

"Barack...always promised me an interesting journey," she wrote.

Her book was partly dedicated to "Malia and Sasha, my two most precious peas."

Longtime Obama family friend Oprah Winfrey moderated Michelle's Chicago book-tour stop.

appearances," adds Mrs. Obama. "They made excellent ambassadors, impervious to criticism and unaware of their own fame."

In *Becoming*'s epilogue, the former first lady looks ahead to her future—and makes it crystal clear what it most definitely will not include. "Because people often ask, I'll say it here directly: I have no intention of running for office, ever. I've never been a fan of politics, and my experience over the last ten years has done little to change that." Though disappointing to many, Mrs. Obama repeated her stance many times during her sold-out 31-city international book tour in 2018-2019, which brought her to NYC, LA, Chicago, London and more for Q&A sessions moderated by the likes of Oprah Winfrey, Reese Witherspoon, Sarah Jessica Parker, Jimmy Kimmel, Stephen Colbert and Rachael Ray. "Eight years is enough," she admitted to Conan O'Brien in an interview on his podcast in March 2019. "It is enough. It's time for new ideas and people.... We need fresh, real, clear eyes in this stuff."

As for herself, Michelle intends to focus on her new phase of life and all its undemanding excitement. "For the first time in many years, I'm unhooked from any obligation as a political spouse, unencumbered by other people's expectations. I have two nearly grown daughters who need me less than they once did. I have a husband who no longer carries the weight of the nation on his shoulders. The responsibilities I've felt—to Sasha and Malia, to Barack, to my career and my country—have shifted in ways that allow me to think differently about what comes next. I've had more time to reflect, to simply be myself.... I am still in progress, and I hope that I always will be." ○

A mural of Michelle by artist Royyal Dog was unveiled in Chicago in August 2019.

LASTING IMPRESSION Michelle made designer Jason Wu a household name when she donned this white chiffon gown at the first inaugural ball in January 2009.

Best Dressed

MICHELLE OBAMA BROKE THE MOLD ON FIRST FASHION.

From the moment her husband was elected president, the world took note of Mrs. Obama's sense of style—perhaps too much. "When I wore flats instead of heels, it got reported in the news," she writes in her memoir's Becoming More section. "My pearls, my belts, my cardigans, my off-the-rack dresses from J.Crew... all seemed to trigger a slew of opinions and instant feedback.... My clothes mattered more to people than anything I had to say." But with fashionistas watching her every outfit, she made it a point to give them something to talk about. She and her wardrobe stylist, Meredith Koop, would spend hours a few times a month going through racks of clothes and "pairing outfits with whatever was on my schedule in the coming weeks." Michelle—who's quick to note she paid for her clothes and accessories, except for formal events—did her best to be "somewhat unpredictable." "It was a thin line to walk: I was supposed to stand out without overshadowing others, to blend in but not fade away," she explains. "I'd match a high-end Michael Kors skirt with a T-shirt from Gap. I wore something from Target one day and Diane von Furstenberg the next. I wanted to draw attention to and celebrate American designers, most especially those who were less established.... For me, my choices were simply a way to use my curious relationship with the public gaze to boost a diverse set of up-and-comers."

LADY IN RED Michelle again turned to Jason Wu for the second inaugural, when she wore this ruby chiffon gown at the 2013 ball.

VIVE LA FRANCE! At a 2014 White House state dinner for French President François Hollande, she wore a dramatic Carolina Herrera gown.

AMERICAN QUEEN The first lady looked more like royalty in a silk Tom Ford at the State Banquet at Buckingham Palace in 2011.

STRIKING MIDNIGHT In 2015, the first lady welcomed China's president Xi Jinping in a Vera Wang–designed off-the-shoulder black vision.

STAY GOLD
For the 2016 Phoenix Awards Dinner, FLOTUS wore a shimmering gown designed by Naeem Khan with hand-painted gold leaf over black tulle.

CIAO, BELLA
For the Italian State Dinner in 2016 (the last one the Obamas hosted), the first lady stunned in an Atelier Versace rose-gold chain mail gown.

SLEEK STATEMENT
At the British State Dinner with Prime Minister David Cameron in 2012, Michelle looked elegant in this gown by Marchesa, adding a Tom Binns statement necklace.

TRUE BLUE
In 2015, she showed off her arms in a strapless Tadashi Shoji gown at the Black Caucus Foundation.

BOLD & BEAUTIFUL
She made a statement in Alexander McQueen for the 2011 China State Dinner.

The first lady and president celebrated Easter 2015 with daughters Malia and Sasha, as well as dogs Sunny and Bo.

PRIDE & JOY

A LOOK INTO OBAMA'S CLOSE RELATIONSHIP WITH THE APPLES OF HIS EYE: HIS DAUGHTERS, MALIA AND SASHA.

He grew up without a father, so Barack Obama was determined not to let history repeat itself "and that my own children would have a father they could count on." But as his career took off, he discovered that juggling fatherhood and the demands of being a politician to be nearly impossible. "In the most basic sense, I've succeeded," he wrote in his 2005 book, *The Audacity of Hope*, of daughters Malia and Sasha, who were then 7 and 4 years old, respectively. "I attend parent-teacher conferences and dance recitals, and my daughters bask in my adoration. And yet, of all the areas of my life, it is in my capacities as a husband and father that I entertain the most doubt."

Indeed, his wife, Michelle, often had to be both mother and father to the girls as Obama's work kept him away from the family home for long stretches—but he always tried to make up for it. "When I'm not out of town, I try to be home for dinner, to hear from Malia and Sasha about their day, to read to them and tuck them into bed," he said in 2005 when he was in the Illinois Senate. "I try not to schedule appearances on Sundays, and in the summers, I'll use the day to take the girls to the zoo or the pool; in the winters, we might visit a museum or the aquarium." Still, doubt always crept in. "Sometimes, when I listen to Michelle talk about her father, I hear the echo of such joy in her, the love and respect that Fraser Robinson earned not through fame or spectacular deeds but through small, daily, ordinary acts—a love he earned by being there. And I ask myself whether my daughters will be able to speak of me in that same way."

Growing up, Obama attended only two birthday parties, so with Malia and Sasha, he made sure their celebrations were special days filled with lots of love—but no presents from Mom and Dad. "We want to teach some limits to them," he explained in 2008. "And their friends bring over presents." Sasha's sixth birthday, especially, stands out to Obama, because he was able to help his wife organize the youngster's party. His duty: Order enough balloons, pizza and ice for 20 children. "I found a place that sold balloons near the gymnastics studio, where the party would be held, and a pizza place that promised delivery at 3:45 p.m.," he later boasted. "By the time the guests showed up the next day, the balloons were in place and the juice boxes were on ice."

Because Obama spent so much time away from his daughters—in 2008, he estimated, "The last 17 months, I've been on the road 98 percent of the time"—when they were all together, it was tough to be the disciplinarian. But lucky for him and Michelle, their girls rarely gave them trouble, aside from not wanting to do chores. That meant the time he did get to spend with them was fun and lighthearted. Sasha, whom Michelle has described as "sassy," once teased her father about his thinning hair. "Well, you have no teeth," he joked back after she had been visited by the Tooth Fairy. As for his eldest, she held her dad accountable for his forgetfulness when it came to her allowance. "Malia will say, 'Hey, you owe me 10 weeks!'" he revealed while campaigning for president. "Originally, we were giving her a dollar a week, as long as she did all her chores. It turns out that she's been doing her chores even without prompting from the allowance, which makes me feel guilty that she's been carrying on her end of the bargain and I haven't been as consistent."

"I THINK ANY YOUNG MAN WHO HAS THE GUTS TO GET THROUGH SECRET SERVICE DESERVES A HEARING."

—Barack Obama, on his daughters dating

"Just like her father, she is an avid reader," Michelle has said of Malia, here with Obama in July 2009.

After years of having a part-time dad as the senator shuttled between Washington, D.C., and Chicago, once the Obamas moved into the White House, the family's home life became more idyllic, thanks in part to a new member. For years, the girls had been asking for a dog, and they finally got their wish once their father was elected. In his November 2008 acceptance speech, the president-elect made a promise to Malia and Sasha. "I love you both so much, and you have earned the new puppy that's coming with us to the White House." After thorough research on breeds (Malia has allergies, so the canine would need to be hypoallergenic), the family settled on a Portuguese Water Dog.

Obama declined to speak at Malia's high school graduation in 2016 because he knew he'd be too emotional and would cry.

First Dogs

Bo and Sunny were popular additions to the White House. "Everybody wants to take pictures," Michelle said.

When Malia and Sasha became first daughters, the only thing they wanted was a puppy. They'd asked for years—and just months after moving into the White House their wish came true with a Portuguese Water Dog they named Bo (after musician Bo Diddley). Before he outgrew the puppy stage, Bo was featured in a number of children's books and as a stuffed animal.

During the family's second term, the White House got more lively when the Obamas added another PWD puppy, Sunny, "a free-spirited rambler who seemed to see no point in being house-trained," Michelle joked in her book *Becoming*. Although Bo and Sunny were rambunctious, they were a great distraction from the stress of presidential life. "They were living, loafing proof that the White House was a home," added Michelle.

The dogs were also perfect ambassadors. "In the evenings, I'd find memos in my briefing book asking me to approve a 'Bo and Sunny Drop-By,' allowing the dogs to mingle with members of the media or children coming for a tour." And when Michelle read *'Twas The Night Before Christmas* at the Children's National Medical Center in 2012, she brought Bo. As she was about to open the book, the 3-year-old pup jumped on her lap—which he was too big for. As the audience laughed, Michelle explained, "This is exactly what he does at home. He tries to beat Malia and Sasha to my lap."

Clockwise from top left: The dogs were in high demand for photos and frequent meet-and-greets; Sunny joined the Obama family in August 2013; Sasha and Bo showed off their "high five" during a visit to D.C.'s Children's National Medical Center in December 2009; Bo quickly bonded with the entire Obama family, but especially the girls.

Barack, Sasha, Michelle and Malia sat for this family portrait in the Green Room at the White House on September 1, 2009.

"I'M INSPIRED BY MY OWN CHILDREN, HOW FULL THEY MAKE MY HEART.... THEY MAKE ME WANT TO BE A BETTER MAN."

—Barack Obama

Beautiful Minds

With Harvard Law grads as parents, the chances were good that Malia and Sasha would be just as brilliant. As first daughters, they studied at Sidwell Friends, a $40,000-a-year Quaker school with a competitive admissions process. When Malia graduated in 2016, her proud father had to wear sunglasses to hide his tears. "He and the first lady are enormously proud of their daughter's accomplishments," said White House Press Secretary Josh Earnest.

Malia took a "gap year," and following an internship at Weinstein Company in New York City, the budding filmmaker enrolled at Harvard in 2017. She quickly assimilated, moving into a dorm and tailgating with friends before the Harvard-Yale football game.

Malia's sister became a freshman in 2019 at the University of Michigan, known for its excellence in engineering, medicine, law, business and economics. Her UM classmates have described Sasha as "a normal student," but she did stick out during orientation: She was surrounded by Secret Service.

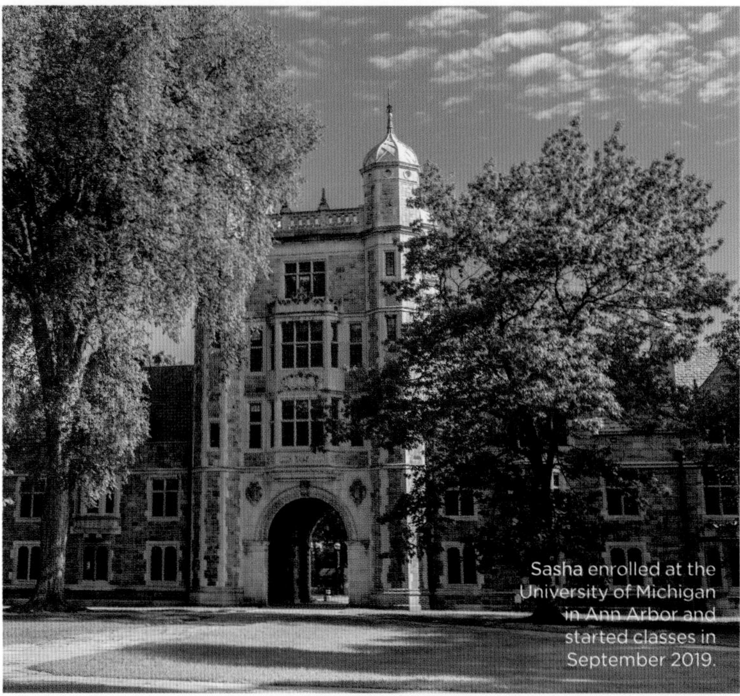

Sasha enrolled at the University of Michigan in Ann Arbor and started classes in September 2019.

Malia goes to Harvard, where both her parents attended law school. She's expected to graduate in 2021.

President Obama and an elegant Malia chatted before a State Dinner for Canadian Prime Minister Justin Trudeau in March 2016.

In April 2009, Senator Ted Kennedy gifted the family with 6-month-old Bo. In photos from his first day at his new home, Malia and Sasha can be seen frolicking with their adorable puppy on the White House's South Lawn. When the president spoke to the press about the first dog, 7-year-old Sasha could barely contain her excitement as she interrupted with a special report on her new furry friend. "He doesn't know how to swim," she adorably told reporters.

As first daughters, it would have been easy for Malia and Sasha to become spoiled by their father's power and living in a palace like the White House, with staff at their beck and call—but the girls turned out quite the opposite, thanks to their parents. The president and first lady adhered to a strict set of rules comprised of dinner at 6:30 p.m., making their beds every morning, cleaning their rooms, and no TV, internet or cellphones from Monday to Friday. And there was no slacking once school let out for the summer. In 2016, *The Boston Globe* reported that 15-year-old Sasha was working the takeout window at Nancy's, a seafood restaurant in Martha's Vineyard—accompanied by Secret Service agents, no less. Of course, there were also lots of perks that came with being the president's daughter. Throughout their eight years in the White House, Malia and Sasha got to rub elbows with many of their favorite stars, like Beyoncé, Jay-Z, the Jonas Brothers and Ryan Reynolds.

In return, the first daughters kept their father grounded. When Obama received the news he had won the Nobel Peace Prize in 2009, he recalled, "Malia walked in and said '...*And* it is Bo's birthday!' And then Sasha added, 'Plus we have a three-day weekend coming up.' So it's good to have kids to keep things in perspective." For his 50th birthday in 2011, Michelle and the girls celebrated the patriarch with a roast. "Each one of them read something, and Malia and Sasha had written out why I am such a wonderful dad," he shared. "And one of the items on Malia's list was, 'You are just the right amount of embarrassing.'"

As lovely as Malia and Sasha grew up to be, the proud father insisted, "Michelle gets all the credit. They don't have an attitude, they're courteous and kind to everybody. They work hard—they don't feel like they're entitled to anything." During that same interview on Ellen DeGeneres's talk show in February 2016, the president got emotional about Malia leaving to attend Harvard, which she did in 2017 after taking a "gap year" to travel. Obama said he wasn't ready for his eldest to fly the coop, even though the mature teenager was. "She's one of my best friends, and it's going to be hard for me not to have her around all the time."

As the Obamas prepared to leave the White House in January 2017, former first daughters Jenna and Barbara Bush shared some advice for Malia and Sasha—just as they had eight years earlier when they gave the Obama girls a tour of their new home (and even taught them how to slide down the banister). "You will be writing the story of your lives, beyond the shadow of your famous parents," the twins wrote in an open letter. "Enjoy college. As most of the world knows, we did. And you won't have the weight of the world on your young shoulders anymore. Explore your passions. Learn who you are. Make mistakes..."

The sacrifices Malia and Sasha made so their father could achieve his dream of becoming the first African American president were certainly not lost on Obama. During his farewell address, he acknowledged their role and gushed about their character. "Malia and Sasha, under the strangest of circumstances, you have become two amazing young women. You are smart and you are beautiful, but more importantly, you are kind and you are thoughtful and you are full of passion. You wore the burden of years in the spotlight so easily. Of all that I've done in my life, I am most proud to be your dad."

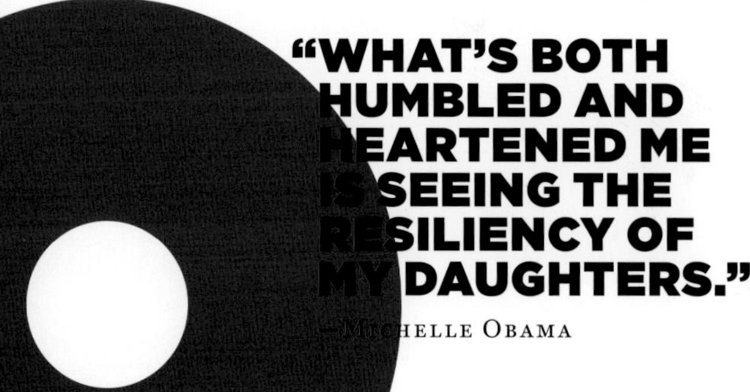

"WHAT'S BOTH HUMBLED AND HEARTENED ME IS SEEING THE RESILIENCY OF MY DAUGHTERS."

—Michelle Obama

President Obama jokes around with his daughters during the annual turkey pardoning ceremony in the Rose Garden on November 25, 2015.

A NEW BEGINNING

IN HIS LIFE AFTER THE WHITE HOUSE, OBAMA HAS ENJOYED SPENDING TIME WITH FAMILY, MEETING WITH FOREIGN DIGNITARIES, WRITING HIS NEXT BOOK AND GETTING BACK TO HIS ROOTS IN COMMUNITY ORGANIZING.

When Barack Obama awoke on January 21, 2017, the day after he turned the presidency and the White House over to Donald Trump, he did something he hadn't during his eight years in office. "I slept in," he revealed in an interview with David Letterman, "which I was pretty happy about.... I sort of enjoyed puttering around the house, finding out, 'Does the coffee maker work?' and fighting with Michelle for closet space."

After leaving 1600 Pennsylvania Avenue, the Obamas (and their dogs, Bo and Sunny) didn't move too far away. Instead of returning to their native Chicago, the family headed just two miles north, to Washington, D.C.'s upscale Kalorama neighborhood, where they settled into a $8.1 million, nine-bedroom, eight-and-a-half-bathroom brick Tudor mansion, to be in close proximity to younger daughter Sasha's Sidwell Friends School. (In June 2019, the 18-year-old graduated and headed to the University of Michigan that fall, while big sister Malia, 21, entered her third year at Harvard University.)

Obama won a friendly kitesurfing contest against Richard Branson.

With his home base in place, Obama looked ahead to the next stage of his life—as an American civilian. "The stereotype of former presidents is, you're kind of sitting around your house, waiting for someone to call, lonely, don't know what to do," he revealed to Letterman in 2018, "but the truth is, it felt exciting." And it certainly looked to be the case: After leaving the White House, the Obamas relished some much-deserved time off, first golfing in Palm Springs, California, before heading to British billionaire Sir Richard Branson's private island in the British Virgin Islands, where the former president kitesurfed. The couple then enjoyed nearly a month in French Polynesia, including a yacht ride aboard

When Obama went kitesurfing in the British Virgin Islands in February 2017, it was the first time the Hawaii native had enjoyed any water sports since becoming president.

Obama was the very first guest on David Letterman's Netflix show, *My Guest Needs No Introduction*, in January 2018.

"WHAT I REALIZED IS THE THING I COULD DO UNIQUELY IS WORK TO TRAIN THE NEXT GENERATION OF LEADERS."

—BARACK OBAMA, ON HIS POST-PRESIDENCY GOALS

entertainment mogul David Geffen's vessel, *The Rising Sun*, with the likes of Bruce Springsteen, Tom Hanks and longtime friend Oprah Winfrey.

After a few months "off," Obama made his first public appearance on April 24, 2017, when he led a discussion with high school and college students at the University of Chicago, where he once taught constitutional law. "So, what's been going on while I've been gone?" he joked. Although he urged them to participate in political life, especially if they were unhappy with the current state of the country, he refrained from talking about Trump—much to the chagrin of Democrats, who implored him to speak up as the new president reversed Obama-era environmental protections, banned travel from predominantly Muslim countries and even accused his predecessor of being behind national-security leaks (see page 170 for more on Trump and Obama). "The single most important thing I can do," Obama told them, is to "help in any way I can prepare the next generation of leadership to take up the baton and to take their own crack at changing the world."

A few weeks later, on May 7, Obama received the Profile in Courage Award "for his enduring commitment to democratic ideals and elevating the standard of political courage" from the John F. Kennedy Presidential Library and Museum. And although he still refused to speak directly about Trump's policies, he did use his acceptance speech to ask lawmakers to show "courage" in the battle over health care as the president fought to end Obamacare. "I hope that current members of Congress recall that it actually doesn't take a lot of courage to aid those who are already powerful, already comfortable, already influential," stated Obama. "But it does require some courage to champion the vulnerable and the sick and the infirm, those who often have no access to the corridors of power."

Obama then headed overseas for a number of appearances—first stopping in Italy to play tourist with Michelle for a few days. In Berlin, he gave a speech alongside German Chancellor Angela Merkel, a longtime friend and ally, to mark the 500th anniversary of the country's Protestant Reformation. It was then on to England for a summit with Prince Harry at Kensington Palace to discuss mental health, conservation and support for veterans. Before his next stop in South Korea to meet with President Moon Jae-in, the entire Obama family spent 10 days in Bali, where they explored temples and botanical gardens and even went white-water rafting.

Obama concluded his first year out of office with another international trip, this time for business, to meet with foreign dignitaries. While in China, he spoke at the Global Alliance of SMEs Summit in Shanghai and convened with President Xi Jinping in Beijing. In India, he had lunch with Prime Minster Narendra Modi and held a town hall gathering for young leaders, organized by his Obama Foundation. His five-day trip came to a close on December 2 in France, where the former POTUS met with President

Obamas & Bushes

A FRIENDSHIP THAT KNOWS NO POLITICAL BOUNDS

During the 2008 election, Obama took shots at then-President George W. Bush—but once he sat in the Oval Office, his opinion changed. In 2013, Obama looked back at the transition from the Bush administration to his own, and noted Bush "couldn't have been nicer to my team and family."

Over the years, the friendship evolved. "To know the man is to like the man," Obama has said of Bush Jr., which holds true for Michelle, too. She and Bush hugged at the opening of the Smithsonian National Museum of African American History in September 2016. "She kind of likes my sense of humor," Bush explained.

Tragedy brought them together again after Bush matriarch Barbara's death and at Senator John McCain's funeral in 2018, when Bush passed Michelle a cough drop during the service. At his father's funeral three months later, Bush again slipped a cough drop into Michelle's hand, which brought a smile to her face. "I love him to death," she's gushed. "He's a wonderful man."

"We just took to each other," George W. Bush said about his affection for Michelle Obama.

On His Successor

WHAT DOES OBAMA THINK ABOUT PRESIDENT DONALD TRUMP?

Before Trump was elected in November 2016, he and Obama shared a tense history, dating back to 2011 when *The Apprentice* star began questioning Obama's birthplace and the legitimacy of his presidency. But once Trump was in the White House, Obama remained silent—until mid-2018. That June, Obama urged the audience at a Democratic National Committee fundraiser to make their voices heard with their vote in 2020: "A majority of the American people prefer a country that comes together rather than being divided."

The following month, Obama again hinted at his feelings on Trump, specifically his stance on immigrants—yet he never uttered the president's name. It wasn't until a September speech at the University of Illinois at Urbana-Champaign that Obama finally mentioned Trump. Although he warned that the POTUS was a "threat to our democracy" who rose to power by "tapping into America's dark history of racial and ethnic and religious division," Obama added he was merely "a symptom, not the cause. It did not start with Donald Trump. He's just capitalizing on resentments that politicians have been fanning for years, a fear and anger that's rooted in our past."

Since becoming president, Trump has continued to blast Obama publicly and on Twitter.

Obama at a 2018 rally in Las Vegas with Senate candidate Jacky Rosen (right).

"IF YOU DON'T LIKE WHAT'S GOING ON RIGHT NOW—AND YOU SHOULDN'T—DON'T COMPLAIN...VOTE!"

—Barack Obama, speaking at a Las Vegas rally

Obama gave a eulogy at John McCain's September 2018 funeral, at the request of the Republican senator.

Obama spoke to more than 50 mayors during the North American Climate Summit in Chicago on December 5, 2017.

Emmanuel Macron, whom he had endorsed months earlier in the country's election.

Back in America, 2018 brought about more exciting opportunities. Both Barack and Michelle inked book deals with Penguin Random House, reportedly worth upwards of $60 million, with a "significant portion" being donated to their Obama Foundation. Michelle released *Becoming* in November of that year, while Barack's post-White House memoir—the first draft of which he wrote by hand on legal pads—is expected to hit shelves during the 2020 presidential election. His book reportedly will cover his life from the 2004 Democratic National Convention through the end of his presidency.

While Obama continued to refrain from making too many statements critical of President Trump, he did speak at John McCain's funeral in September 2018, at the request of the late Arizona senator. Obama used his eulogy to call out the rancor in public discourse since Trump took office, describing it as "small and mean and petty." Said Obama, "It's a politics that pretends to be brave and tough, but in fact is born of fear." Not long after delivering his eulogy, Obama also criticized Trump's decision to rescind the Deferred Action for Childhood Arrivals immigration policy in a Facebook post, saying, "To target these young people is wrong—because they have done nothing wrong."

More recently, Obama has been focusing on plans for his presidential library (see page 172), his and Michelle's producing deal with Netflix (see page 182) and he's gone back to his roots of community organizing. As he looked ahead to the future, he called on his social media followers to "make a commitment: find something you want to change in your community and take the first step toward changing it." ○

"THIS IS NOT THE APOCALYPSE.... I THINK NOTHING IS THE END OF THE WORLD UNTIL THE END OF THE WORLD."

—Barack Obama, on Donald Trump's presidency

"WE PROVED THAT WE ARE STILL A PEOPLE CAPABLE OF DOING BIG THINGS AND TACKLING OUR BIGGEST CHALLENGES."

—Barack Obama, after Congress passed the Affordable Care Act

The museum's form is inspired by four hands coming together.

THE LEGACY CONTINUES

THE BARACK OBAMA PRESIDENTIAL CENTER IN CHICAGO HAS BEEN YEARS IN THE MAKING, BUT THE $500 MILLION LIBRARY AND MUSEUM WILL BE WELL WORTH THE WAIT.

To celebrate his historic presidency, Barack Obama is honoring the city that first gave him an opportunity: Chicago. Just four months after his second term ended, Barack and Michelle unveiled the first look at the Obama Presidential Center, an architectural beauty with a modern design to match its distinction of being the first completely digital presidential library in the country. "All the strands of my life came together and I really became a man when I moved to Chicago," Obama explained. "That's where I was able to apply that early idealism to try to work in communities in public service. That's where I met my wife. That's where my children were born." The development of his presidential center has been both a passion project and labor of love.

Located in Jackson Park, on the city's South Side, the 225,000-square-foot complex is comprised of four main buildings: an eight-story museum, a two-story forum, a 5,000-square-foot branch of the Chicago Public Library and a sports facility. Beyond the epicenter, the vibrant 20-acre campus also includes a public plaza; a lush promenade with scenic walking paths and a hill for sledding in the winter; a Women's Garden; a Wetland Walk; a Great Lawn; and a 2-acre Children's Play Area featuring an interactive playground for four seasons of fun and exploration. "It's not just a building," says Obama. "It's not just a park. Hopefully it's a hub where all of us can see a brighter future for the South Side."

Anchored at the north end of the property, the towering museum—the embodiment of hope—is a light-colored stone structure described as the "lantern" of the center. Its design is just as significant: the idea of ascension, like Obama's rise from Illinois senator to president of the United States. Inside the 165,000-square-foot space, the exhibits showcase that progression—and in a most unique way, as Obama didn't want the museum to be a place "kids are being dragged to for a field trip."

The ground floor is "the starting point of the narrative that made the President Obama story possible," explains museum director Louise Bernard, including "the moments, milestones in U.S. history that would lead to the election of the first African American president." The second level is dedicated to Obama's two terms in office and life in the White House. On the third floor, visitors will learn about the West and East Wings and the people who worked

In May 2017, Obama unveiled plans for his Obama Presidential Center in Chicago.

there behind the scenes during his administration. The fourth floor is home to a full-scale exact replica of Obama's Oval Office (which the public can also explore via virtual reality). And at the very top, the Sky Room offers a place to reflect on it all, with panoramic views of Chicago and Lake Michigan.

"The Obamas want to create a safe, warm, inviting place that brings people in, teaches them something new and inspires them to create change in their own communities," adds Martin Nesbitt, chair of the Obama Foundation. "The Center will be a place for doing, not just looking or listening." And visitors will experience it all in a most unique presentation: entirely digitally. The majority of artifacts from Obama's presidency—1.5 billion pages of emails, PDFs, documents and spreadsheets—were "born digital" (meaning there was never a paper version), so that's exactly how museum patrons will digest them.

The local South Side community is the heart of the forum. Designed to bring people together, the space will be free to the public and home to numerous collaborative and creative spaces, such as an auditorium; a broadcast and recording studio; flexible learning and meeting spaces; as well as a restaurant with outdoor seating. At the library, learning comes to life with an interactive digital media space. On the roof sits a garden similar to the one Michelle famously planted at the White House and where guests will be encouraged to get their hands dirty and learn about fruits and vegetables and how to grow them. As first lady, nutrition and physical activity were tenets of her Let's Move! campaign, and the center's public sports facility encourages athletics and recreation—and it even includes a nod to her husband's favorite pastime, basketball.

Construction on the Obama Center was slated to begin in late 2018 for a 2021 opening, but opposition from local public parks activists significantly delayed groundbreaking (see below for more). Finally in June 2019, a judge ruled in favor of the Obamas—giving them hope for what they believe will change their beloved community. "Our vision for the Obama Presidential Center has always been one where the location reinforces the project's core aims, a celebration of history, a place of connection, engagement for the public, and an investment in community," says Obama Foundation CEO David Simas. "We couldn't be more excited to move forward on our plans, arm-in-arm with our neighbors in Chicago, ready to bring investment and jobs to the South Side."

The museum building will anchor the north end of the plaza.

The Battle With Chicago

Although the Obama Presidential Center promises to be a boon to Chicago—it's estimated to create thousands of jobs and infuse $3.1 million into the local economy in its first decade of operation—not everyone in the community was supportive. Opponents criticized the City of Chicago for what they called a "massive giveaway" of public land worth millions of dollars to the Obama Foundation. Preservationist groups joined in, claiming the area designated for the center could affect Jackson Park's status on the National Register of Historic Places (it dates back to 1893). And in May 2018, a year after Obama unveiled his project, Protect Our Parks filed a lawsuit to block its development. Over the next year, city lawyers battled it out in federal court as progress on the center came to a standstill. In June 2019, Judge Robert Blakey ultimately dismissed the lawsuit, ruling, "The facts do not warrant a trial and construction should commence without delay."

POWER COUPLE

BARACK AND MICHELLE OBAMA MAY NOT BE IN THE WHITE HOUSE ANY MORE, BUT THEY'RE EVEN MORE INSPIRING AS AMERICAN CIVILIANS.

Michelle and Barack showed off their dance moves while Beyoncé sang "At Last" at the first Inaugural ball in 2009.

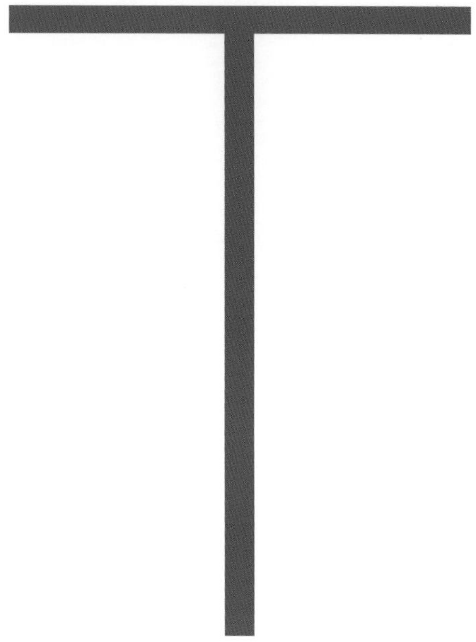

The work didn't end for Barack and Michelle Obama once they left the White House—it was only the beginning. In the years since the world knew them best as the president and first lady, the first couple has evolved into the ultimate power couple: Obama Foundation ambassadors, global leaders, activists, mentors, even Oscar-winning producers. "The [White] House didn't define us," Michelle said in a 2020 interview with Oprah Winfrey. "It's the values that defined us."

At the Obama Foundation, their Chicago-based nonprofit organization, the core principles are team, humility, integrity, inclusivity, stewardship, fearlessness and imagination. Following popular summits all over the U.S., Barack and Michelle took their initiative international, culminating in a weeklong event in Kuala Lumpur, Malaysia, in December 2019 for 200 emerging world leaders from 33 different nations and territories across the Asia Pacific region. Workshops included entrepreneurship, skill-building and leadership, with a focus on the future.

In separate talks, the Obamas opened up about life lessons from their personal journeys: Barack sat down with his sister Maya Soetoro-Ng to discuss growing up in Indonesia and Hawaii, while Michelle spoke with Julia Roberts and Blondie singer Deborah Harry about women's issues and even got candid about her nearly 30-year marriage. "It's a hard thing," she revealed. "Barack and I understood that about each other. There was counseling for us. We learned that we have to work through challenging times. We worked at getting marriage counseling because sometimes we can't do this on our own. A relationship requires a community to get through. Marriage is not a solo expedition. You need a friend, family member or outside help."

Barack and Michelle have always been open about her struggle in the spotlight as first lady. But years away from the White House, her freedom not only has empowered her, but more so the complicated relationship with her husband. "I was one of those wives who was like, 'I'm taking you to marriage counseling so *you* can be fixed, Barack Obama, because *I'm* perfect,'" Michelle told *Tonight Show* host Jimmy Fallon during one stop on her book tour for *Becoming*. "I was like, 'Dr. X please fix him.' But marriage counseling was a turning point for me understanding that it wasn't up to my husband to make me happy. I had to learn how to fill myself up and put myself higher on my priority list."

Barack, for his part, has made no secret of his love and appreciation for his wife, despite their occasional difficulties. "Obviously, I couldn't have done anything that I've done without Michelle," he told Winfrey before his presidency ended. "She is just my rock. I count on her in so many ways every single day."

Since leaving the White House, their bond has continued to flourish. For their wedding anniversary in October 2019, they both posted loving messages celebrating the occasion. "Like the Beatles said: It's getting better all the time. Thanks, babe, for 27 amazing years," Barack tweeted. Michelle responded with a photo of the two of them: "27 years ago, this guy promised me a life full of adventure. I'd say he's delivered. Here's to our next chapter of becoming empty nesters and discovering what's next—while still feeling

Michelle and Barack waved to the audience at the opening of the Obama Foundation Summit on October 29, 2019.

The former first couple took part in an Obama Foundation community service event in Kuala Lumpur, Malaysia, in December 2019.

"IT'S USEFUL TO REMIND OURSELVES THAT THERE ARE A BUNCH OF DIFFERENT WAYS TO HAVE AN IMPACT."

—Barack Obama

Obama's Elegant Homes

For U.S. presidents, the White House's 132 rooms and 36 bathrooms come with the job. That kind of luxury is no doubt hard to leave behind, and when the Obamas moved out in 2017, they stayed close, paying $8.1 million for an 8,200-square-foot house in the nearby Kalorama neighborhood of Washington. Youngest daughter Sasha may have scored the best spot in the eight-bedroom, nine-and-a-half bath red brick home. "She has this two-room suite," Michelle told Ellen DeGeneres. Barack, however, "doesn't have enough closet space." He might now: For seven out of eight years in office, the Obamas spent vacations on Martha's Vineyard. In December 2019, they doubled down, reportedly purchasing a $11.75 million, seven-bedroom mansion that sits on 29 acres of waterfront property near Edgartown. While many presidents have vacationed on the tony Massachusetts island, Obama is the first former POTUS to buy property there.

The Obamas also visited Martha's Vineyard when Barack was a senator.

The Obamas may have chosen their D.C. home for its proximity to Malia and Sasha's Sidwell Friends School.

"WHEN YOU'VE WORKED HARD, AND WALKED THROUGH THAT DOORWAY OF OPPORTUNITY, YOU DO NOT SLAM IT SHUT BEHIND YOU."

—MICHELLE OBAMA

Other homeowners on Martha's Vineyard include David Letterman and Meg Ryan.

A former whaling port, Edgartown has many historic homes.

the magic that brought us together all those years ago. Happy anniversary, Barack."

And their newly empty nest seems only to have strengthened their relationship. Following the departure of their girls for college—Malia started Harvard in 2017 and Sasha matriculated at the University of Michigan in the fall of 2019—the couple is finally "seeing each other again," Michelle told Winfrey in 2020, just a few months after her youngest daughter left home. "Parenting takes up a lot of emotional space. Raising a family together is a hard thing. It takes a toll. But if you're with the person, if you know why you are with them. You understand that there was a friendship and a foundation there," Michelle explained. "You can have chunks of hard, bad times and if that's how you define your marriage by just the hard times, then you'll miss the truth of what's really there."

During the same interview, Winfrey—who has known the couple since before Barack was elected president—noted that every time she's seen the couple together since 2016, they seem better than they ever have been. And Michelle agreed. "We are happy people, but why wouldn't we be?" she replied. "We have our health. We have each other. We have a sense of purpose. I mean, there are things to complain about, but we—the two of us—we don't have anything to complain about. That's why we believe we owe so much, because to whom much is given, much is expected."

Producing Partners

Steven Bognar, Julia Reichert and Jeff Reichert accepted the Oscar for *American Factory.*

A little over a year after leaving the White House, the Obamas added a new title to their résumé: entertainers. The couple established Higher Ground Productions, and in May 2018 signed a multiyear partnership with Netflix to create a diverse mix of content. "I have always believed in the power of storytelling to inspire us, to make us think differently about the world around us, and to help us open our minds and hearts to others," said Michelle.

Judging by their first release, the Obamas are on the right track. *American Factory*, an emotional documentary about the culture clash between Chinese and American workers at a Chinese-owned Ohio automotive glass factory, won Best Documentary Feature at the 2020 Academy Awards.

Also on Higher Ground's slate: *Bloom*, an upstairs/downstairs drama series about the struggles faced by women of color in New York City's fashion world post-World War II; *Overlooked*, a scripted series adapted from *The New York Times*' obituary column about extraordinary people whose deaths weren't reported by the newspaper; *Listen to Your Vegetables & Eat Your Parents*, a program for preschoolers; *Crip Camp*, a documentary about a camp for disabled teenagers located in Woodstock, New York; as well as adaptations of two nonfiction books, *The Fifth Risk: Undoing Democracy* from author Michael Lewis, and the Pulitzer Prize-winning *Frederick Douglass: Prophet of Freedom*.

The Obamas are also getting into podcasts via a partnership with Spotify, even lending their voices to some recordings. "We've always believed in the value of entertaining, thought-provoking conversation," Barack stated. "It helps us build connections with each other and open ourselves up to new ideas."

Michelle and Barack shared a laugh when their official portraits were unveiled at the National Portrait Gallery in 2018.

"MICHELLE'S LIKE BEYONCÉ IN THAT SONG, 'LET ME UPGRADE YA!' SHE UPGRADED ME."

—Barack Obama

Obama admired the portrait of his wife, by Amy Sherald, unveiled along with his own at the National Portrait Gallery in February 2018.

"IF YOU WERE GOING TO NAME THE 100 MOST POPULAR THINGS THAT I HAVE DONE AS PRESIDENT, BEING MARRIED TO MICHELLE OBAMA IS NO. 1."

—Barack Obama

President Obama's official portrait, by Kehinde Wiley, includes flowers that have special meanings for the former POTUS.

E

F

G

H

COVER Kwaku Alston/Getty Images **FRONT FLAP** EMMANUEL DUNAND/Getty Images **2-3** Charles Ommanney/Getty Images **4-5** (From left) Pablo Martinez Monsivais/AP Photo; Polaris; The White House/Handout/Getty Images; John Gress/Getty Images; Handout/Getty Images; ©Netflix/Courtesy Everett Collection **6-7** Jacquelyn Martin/AP/Shutterstock **8-9** White House Photo/Alamy Stock Photo **10** Alex Wong/Getty Images **11** Pool/Getty Images **12-15** American Photo Archive/Alamy Stock Photo (2) **16** (From top) Handout/Getty Images; The White House/Handout/Getty Images **17** Pablo Martinez Monsivais/AP Photo **18** Pool/Getty Images **19** Mark Wilson/Getty Images **20-23** White House Photo/Alamy Stock Photo (3) **24-25** World History Archive/Alamy Stock Photo **26-27** White House Photo/Alamy Stock Photo (2) **28** The White House/Handout/Getty Images **29** (From top) Scott Olson/Getty Images; The White House/Handout/Getty Images **30-31** (From left) The White House/Handout/Getty Images; WPA Pool/Getty Images **32** White House Photo/Alamy Stock Photo **33** The White House/Handout/Getty Images **34-35** (Clockwise from top left) Pool/Getty Images; The White House/Handout/Getty Images (2) **36** White House Photo/Alamy Stock Photo 37 The White House/Handout/Getty Images **38-39** (Clockwise from top left) The White House/Handout/Getty Images (2); Scott Olson/Getty Images **40-41** The White House/Handout/Getty Images **42-43** (Clockwise from left) Kristoffer Tripplaar/Alamy Stock Photo; David McNew/Getty Images; White House Photo/Alamy Stock Photo **44-45** White House Photo/Alamy Stock Photo **46-47** (Clockwise from top left) 506 collection/Alamy Stock Photo; White House Photo/Alamy Stock Photo; The White House/Handout/Getty Images **48** The White House/Handout/Getty Images (2) **49-51** White House Photo/Alamy Stock Photo (2) **53-55** Polaris (2) **57** INS News Agency Ltd./REX/Shutterstock **58-59** Polaris (3) **61** Kyodo/AP Images **62-63** Polaris **64** Laura S. L. Kong/Getty Images **66** Joe Wrinn/Harvard University/Getty Images **68** Polaris **70-71** Joe Wrinn/Harvard University/Getty Images **72** Boston Globe/Getty Images **73** INS News Agency Ltd./REX/Shutterstock **75-77** Polaris (2) **78** INS News Agency Ltd./REX/Shutterstock **79** Scott Olson/Getty Images **80-81** Polaris (2) **83** Nam Y. Huh/AP Photo **85** Charles Ommanney/Getty Images **87** M. Spencer Green/AP Photo **88** (From top) Polaris; Courtesy of Dreams from My Father/Barack Obama **89** Seth Perlman/AP Photo **91** Shawn Thew/EPA/REX/Shutterstock **92** Jed Jacobsohn/Getty Images **93** Courtesy of Time Magazine **94-95** Scott Olson/Getty Images **96-97** Charles Ommanney/Getty Images **99** (Clockwise from top left) Mark Wilson/Getty Images; Scott Olson/Getty Images; HALEY/SIPA/AP Photo; Charles Ommanney/Getty Images **100** (Clockwise from top left) David Lienemann/Getty Images; STAN HONDA/Getty Images; EMMANUEL DUNAND/AFP/Getty Images; SAUL LOEB/Getty Images **102-103** Charles Ommanney/Getty Images **105** (Clockwise from top left) Jae C. Hong/AP Photo; EMMANUEL DUNAND/AFP/Getty Images; SAUL LOEB/AFP/Getty Images; EMMANUEL DUNAND/AFP/Getty Images **106-107** Robert Daemmrich Photography Inc/Getty Images **108** SAUL LOEB/AFP/Getty Images **109** Chicago Tribune/Getty Images **110** TIM SLOAN/AFP/Getty Images **111** NBC NewsWire/Getty Images **112-113** The White House/Handout/Getty Images **115** Logan Mock-Bunting/Getty Images **116** U.S. Navy/Handout/Getty Images **117** Spencer Platt/Getty Images **118** Chip Somodevilla/Getty Images **119** SAUL LOEB/Getty Images **120-121** MANDEL NGAN/Getty Images **122** Mario Tama/Getty Images **124-125** (From left) Staff/Getty Images; MCT/Getty Images **126-127** John Gress/Getty Images **129** MLADEN ANTONOV/Getty Images **130** dpa picture alliance/Alamy Stock Photo **131** Alex Wong/Getty Images **132** (Clockwise from top left) MANDEL NGAN/AFP/Getty Images; YASIN AKGUL/AFP/Getty Images; Win McNamee/Getty Images; dpa picture alliance/Alamy Stock Photo **134-135** American Photo Archive/Alamy Stock Photo **137** Universal History Archive/UIG/Getty Images **138** (Clockwise from top left) Richard Drew/AP/Shutterstock; Joe Raedle/Getty Images; The White House/Handout/Getty Images **140-141** White House Photo/Alamy Stock Photo **142** Jeff J Mitchell/Getty Images **143** (Clockwise from top left) Sandra Baker/Alamy Stock Photo; Polaris; Scott Olson/Getty Images; EMMANUEL DUNAND/AFP/Getty Images; MCT/Getty Images **144-145** Randy Holmes/Walt Disney Television/Getty Images **146** (From top) Win McNamee/Getty Images; NHAC NGUYEN/Getty Images **148** (Clockwise from top left) BRENDAN SMIALOWSKI/AFP/Getty Images; JIM YOUNG/Getty Images; White House Photo/Alamy Stock Photo **149** Raymond Boyd/Getty Images **150** Mark Wilson/Getty Images **151** Michael Kovac/WireImage/Getty Images **152** (From left) Chip Somodevilla/Getty Images; Chris Jackson/Getty Images; dpa picture alliance/Alamy Stock Photo **153** (Clockwise from top left) UPI/Alamy Stock Photo; NICHOLAS KAMM/AFP/Getty Images; Earl Gibson III/Getty Images; JEWEL SAMAD/Getty Images; Carolyn Kaster/AP Photo **154** Handout/Getty Images **156** Pool/Getty Images **157** American Photo Archive/Alamy Stock Photo **158** Handout/Getty Images **159** (Clockwise from top left) JEWEL SAMAD/AFP/Getty Images; Alex Wong/Getty Images; Ron Edmonds/AP/Shutterstock; SAUL LOEB/Getty Images **160-161** Handout/White House/Getty Images **162** (From top) tiny-al/Getty Images; jorgeantonio/Getty Images **163** White House Photo/Alamy Stock Photo **165** Chip Somodevilla/Getty Images **166-167** Jack Brockway/Getty Images (2) **168** ©Netflix/Courtesy Everett Collection **169** ZACH GIBSON/AFP/Getty Images **170-171** (Clockwise from bottom left) Patsy Lynch/Alamy Stock Photo; Ethan Miller/Getty Images; Scott Olson/Getty Images; UPI/Alamy Stock Photo **172** Courtesy of Obama Foundation **174** Scott Olson/Getty Images **175** (From top) Courtesy of Obama Foundation; Chicago Tribune/TNS/Getty Images **177** Mark Wilson/Getty Images **179** (From top) Scott Olson/Getty Images; Vincent Thian/AP/Shutterstock **180-181** (Clockwise from top) dpa picture alliance/Alamy Stock Photo; Maremagnum/Getty Images; Alinn Mihai/Shutterstock; Ron Sachs-Pool/Getty Images **182** (From left) Jennifer Graylock - PA Images/Getty Images; Courtesy of American Factory **183** The Washington Post/Getty Images **184** Mark Wilson/Getty Images **185** Martin Shields/Alamy Stock Photo SPINE David McNew/Getty Images **BACK FLAP** The White House/Handout/Getty Images **BACK COVER** (Clockwise from top left) EMMANUEL DUNAND/AFP/Getty Images; White House Photo/Alamy Stock Photo; American Photo Archive/Alamy Stock Photo; White House Photo/Alamy Stock Photo; Handout/Getty Images; John Gress/Getty Images

An Imprint of
Centennial Media, LLC
40 Worth St., 10th Floor
New York, NY 10013, U.S.A.

CENTENNIAL BOOKS is a trademark of Centennial Media, LLC

ISBN 978-1-951274-27-6

Distributed by
Simon & Schuster, Inc.
1230 Avenue of the Americas
New York, NY 10020, U.S.A.

For information about custom editions, special sales and premium and corporate purchases, please contact Centennial Media at contact@centennialmedia.com.

Manufactured in China

10 9 8 7 6 5 4 3 2

Publishers & Co-Founders Ben Harris, Sebastian Raatz
Editorial Director Annabel Vered
Creative Director Jessica Power
Executive Editor Janet Giovanelli
Deputy Editors Ron Kelly, Alyssa Shaffer
Design Director Ben Margherita
Art Directors Andrea Lukeman, Natali Suasnavas, Joseph Ulatowski
Assistant Art Director Jaclyn Loney
Photo Editor Kim Kuhn
Production Manager Paul Rodina
Production Assistant Alyssa Swiderski
Editorial Assistant Tiana Schippa
Sales & Marketing Jeremy Nurnberg